Christians cannot be healthy if they d
those things that are now unseen. Paul E
drawing us to marvel and wonder at the
majesty and righteousness. May it help i
store!

MICHAEL REEVES
President and Professor of Theology,
Union School of Theology, Oxford

Very soon after Paul had given one of the talks in this book a mother in the church suddenly and unexpectedly died. The anguish and shock was so painful, when it came to the funeral one of her unbelieving relatives told me 'not long at the graveside – it will be too much'. Yet the truth of what Paul Blackham had taught the church was lived out before our eyes. As we lowered her coffin into the grave, there was the most extraordinary peace. I remember a father explaining to his son what the Bible said was happening. I remember seeing many of the members at peace and understanding how the Lord teaches us to grieve and rejoice and I saw and heard that same relative comment on what a remarkable burial it was.

This is what Bible teaching should be. Something lived out in church life bring glory to Jesus. Read the book. Seriously, read the book.

STEVE LEVY
Pastor,
Mount Pleasant Baptist Church, Swansea, Wales

This magnificent book is long, long overdue. In it we hear the warming magnetism of the author's own voice as – from his remarkable knowledge of the whole Bible – he assists us on these deepest questions of life and eternity. Start at the final Appendix, if you like – that alone makes vital reading!

RICHARD BEWES OBE
formerly of All Souls Church,
Langham Place, London

An immensely stimulating read from someone whose ministry reflects the fact he believes these truths to his core! I've been preaching on the subject of Heaven and Hell for over twenty-five years, and yet I found myself learning new things on page after page. I really do believe this is a book that must find its way into the hands of all those who believe the pulpit stands on the edge of eternity.

RICO TICE
Author, *Christianity Explored* & Associate Minister,
at All Souls Church, Langham Place, London

THE
GREAT
UNKNOWN?

WHAT THE BIBLE SAYS
ABOUT HEAVEN AND HELL

PAUL BLACKHAM

CHRISTIAN
FOCUS

Copyright © Paul Blackham 2016

paperback ISBN 978-1-78191-782-4
epub ISBN 978-1-78191-883-8
mobi ISBN 978-1-78191-884-5

10 9 8 7 6 5 4 3 2 1

Published in 2016
by
Christian Focus Publications Ltd,
Geanies House, Fearn, Ross-shire,
IV20 1TW, Great Britain.

www.christianfocus.com

Cover design by Moose77.com

Printed and bound
by
Bell & Bain, Glasgow

MIX
Paper from
responsible sources
FSC® C007785

Contents

Thanks to Mount Pleasant Baptist Church and Steve Levy, for such great kindness and wisdom over the years – and for giving me the chance to study these truths and teach them at the annual House Party.

Introduction

What is the connection between heaven and earth?
Where is paradise and what's it like?
What is death and why does it happen?
What happens to us when we die before that final
day of judgement?
What is the Christian hope?

OVER the years I have been asked many questions about life, the universe and everything. People ask about the existence of God, about suffering and the truth of different religions. However, the question that seems to come up the most is about what happens when we die.

For some people there is a vague feeling that most of us will 'go into the light', or into some vaguely 'better place'. An increasing number of others, perhaps even a majority in the English-speaking world, suspect that there is nothing at all, that death will be a simple oblivion as definite and final as the decay of the corpse. Nevertheless, the question is constantly asked.

Jesus Himself was questioned about life after death by members of a religious cult (the Sadducees). His answer to them was simple:

> Now about the dead rising – have you not read in the Book of Moses, in the account of the burning bush, how God said to him, 'I am the God of Abraham, the God of Isaac, and the God of Jacob'? He is not the God of the dead, but of the living. You are badly mistaken! (Mark 12:26-27)

Jesus says that their questions have already been answered – in the 'Book of Moses'.

The Sadducees believed that there is nothing beyond the physical life of this world – Acts 23:8. They didn't believe in angels or ghosts or any kind of 'floating away into the light' after death. This life is where we see God's blessing or curse, in the good things and the bad things that happen in life. Obviously this was appealing to rich and powerful people, but not so appealing to poor and exploited people.

As we begin, we have to realise that the cult of the Sadducees is not extinct! That kind of thinking is all too common even today. Many assume that blessing or cursing is all about **this** life, and even though many don't point to some kind of god as the explanation, yet they perhaps shrug their shoulders and speak about the luck of the draw or fate or the meaningless brutality of random chance.

This uncertainty about the bigger picture of life, death and eternity can also be felt in churches and Bible study.

Some people today teach that the Old Testament is concerned only with this mortal life and people expected to disappear into the dust when they died with nothing but a possible shadowy, mindless existence in the land of the dead (Sheol). Look at this quote from a current evangelical dictionary!

> Through much of the Old Testament period, it was believed that all went one place, whether human or animal whether righteous or wicked. No one could avoid Sheol which was thought to be down in the lowest parts of the earth.[1]

So let's find out the truth about heaven and hell and life after death – as Moses taught it, just as Jesus told us to do.

In this book we will begin by looking at the teaching of Moses in depth but then go on to look at the former prophets, the latter prophets, the wisdom literature, the gospels, the epistles and the apocalyptic literature. We want to systematically walk through the whole Bible to get a sense of its big picture of heaven and hell.

---

1. Baker, Grand Rapids, 1996.

CHAPTER 1

PARADISE AND THE PRESENCE OF GOD

The wall of fire

Now Moses was tending the flock of Jethro his father-in-law, the priest of Midian, and he led the flock to the far side of the desert and came to Horeb, the mountain of God. There the Angel of the LORD appeared to him in flames of fire from within a bush. Moses saw that though the bush was on fire it did not burn up. So Moses thought, 'I will go over and see this strange sight – why the bush does not burn up.'

When the LORD saw that he had gone over to look, God called to him from within the bush, 'Moses! Moses!'

And Moses said, 'Here I am.'

'Do not come any closer,' God said. 'Take off your sandals, for the place where you are standing is holy ground.' Then he said, 'I am the God of your father, the

God of Abraham, the God of Isaac and the God of Jacob.'
At this, Moses hid his face, because he was afraid to look at
God. (Exod. 3:1-6)

MOSES is confronted by the Angel of the LORD at Mount
Horeb.

If we take a moment to consider this we can see why it
was so significant for Jesus to refer back to this incident.

The word 'angel' means 'one who is sent'. There are hundreds of millions of these creatures in the heavenly realms
(Rev. 5:11). However throughout the Old Testament there
is a unique character called The Angel of the LORD, literally
The One Sent from the LORD.

This has a special significance in the Bible as a whole
because, of course, there is One who is sent from the Father,
sent to do His will in a unique and eternal sense. In John 4:34
Jesus loves to be sent to do His Father's will – 'My food,' said
Jesus, 'is to do the will of him who sent me and to finish his
work.'

Jesus is the One sent from the Father and therefore most
Christians down through history think that The Angel of
the LORD was the LORD Jesus Himself, before He became
flesh, before He was born of Mary.[1]

So, going back to the incident in Exodus chapter 3, the
Angel of the LORD was near to Moses and yet the flames of
fire tell us that there is a serious barrier between them.

---

1. In this book we will sometimes refer to the Eternal Son of the Father
   simply as 'Jesus' – even before He was born of Mary, even while He
   was working in the Old Testament. The Bible itself does this in Jude
   verse 5 and for most readers it makes it easier to understand who we
   are speaking about as the Saviour of His people in all ages.

This barrier between heaven and earth was marked by fire right back in Genesis 3:

> The LORD God banished (Adam) from the Garden of Eden to work the ground from which he had been taken. After he drove the man out, he placed on the east side of the Garden of Eden cherubim and a flaming sword flashing back and forth to guard the way to the tree of life. (Gen. 3:23-24)

Fire guards the barrier between heaven and earth every time a sacrifice is made. Every time a slaughtered animal is thrown into the fire of the altar at the tabernacle, the ancient church of the Old Testament was looking forward to the Lamb of God who would make a permanent way through that fire.

This is vital. The questions of heaven and hell, life and death, are expressed in the fire. The fire that divides heaven and earth not only prevents us from drawing near to the LORD God – it also ensures our death. The day Adam and Eve ate the forbidden fruit and chose an independent life, cut off from God, their death was certain. Once they had unplugged the world from the source of life, from God the Son who is the Light and Life of the whole creation, death was inevitable for all.

Being separated from God means that we are separated from life itself. Sooner or later the small bit of life that has been lent to us ebbs away. It cannot be replaced by anything on this side of the barrier. We might cling on to this bit of borrowed life as tightly as we can, yet even as we grasp it, this life is lost.

Right now we can **exist**, but we can't ever really **live** if we are cut off from the Fountain of Life.

That is what it unavoidably means to be exiled on this side of the wall of fire.

Jesus – the way through the fire

However, God the Son, whose true home and nature is on the other side of the wall of fire, speaks to Moses. Jesus, the Word and voice of the Father, the one through whom all things were made in Genesis chapter 1, confronts Moses from within the mysterious burning flames.

His words are wonderful, good news – 'I **am** the God of your father, the God of Abraham, the God of Isaac and the God of Jacob'.

Though those saints had been dead for more than 400 years, the first thing the Eternal Christ wanted to tell Moses was that Abraham, Isaac and Jacob were alive and well on the other side! It sounds almost too amazing to be true! These men had trusted in Christ throughout their mortal lives on this side of the separating fire, but the LORD God Himself declares that they are still with Him now on the other side of the divide!

We will learn much more about the strong resurrection hope of these ancient church leaders in later chapters. But perhaps what we need to do first of all is get a clear understanding of the other side of that wall of fire.

Heaven

What are the heavens?

What is paradise?

Does the Living God live up in the sky?

Is there any connection between heaven and earth, between **that** side of the separating fire and **this** side of the separating fire?

14

I came across a quotation from Spurgeon the other day that gets us off to the very best start:

> Samuel Rutherford says, 'Heaven and Christ are the same thing'. To be with Christ is to be in heaven, and to be in heaven is to be with Christ. That prisoner of the Lord very sweetly writes in one of his glowing letters – 'O my Lord Jesus Christ, if I could be in heaven without thee, it would be a hell; and if I could be in hell, and have thee still, it would be a heaven to me, for thou art all the heaven I want.' [2]

To live forever in a perfect earthly environment without Jesus would end up being a kind of hell where our deepest desires, our thirst for the Living God, would be forever unsatisfied. To live forever with a raging thirst for God would hardly be eased by even the most pleasant environment. Most of us know what it is to have a sickness of the soul even surrounded by great prosperity and physical comfort.

This is the key to understanding what is going on at the beginning of the world in Genesis. Let's go back to see how the heavens and the earth were made.

An incredible place!

> Now the LORD God had planted a garden in the east, in Eden; and there he put the man he had formed. And the LORD God made all kinds of trees grow out of the ground – trees that were pleasing to the eye and good for food. In the middle of the garden were the tree of life and the tree of the knowledge of good and evil. A river watering the

---

2. *Morning and Evening*, January 17th.

garden flowed from Eden; from there it was separated into four headwaters. (Gen. 2:8-10)

The man and his wife heard the sound (Voice) of the LORD God as he was walking in the garden in the cool of the day, and they hid from the LORD God among the trees of the garden. But the LORD God called to the man, 'Where are you?' He answered, 'I heard you in the garden, and I was afraid.' (Gen. 3:8-10)

The LORD God made garments of skin for Adam and his wife and clothed them. And the LORD God said, 'The man has now become like one of us, knowing good and evil. He must not be allowed to reach out his hand and take also from the tree of life and eat, and live forever.' So the LORD God banished him from the Garden of Eden to work the ground from which he had been taken. After he drove the man out, he placed on the east side of the Garden of Eden cherubim and a flaming sword flashing back and forth to guard the way to the tree of life. (Gen. 3:21-24)

Cain went out from the LORD's presence and lived in the land of Nod, east of Eden. (Gen. 4:16)

These passages are the foundation to the Bible's story. The Garden of Eden – which is also referred to as paradise and the garden of God – is the centrepiece for the newly created universe.

This paradise is an incredible place. It is good for us to study this carefully because it is the base line for all our hopes. Although the new creation future takes that paradise to even higher levels of glory, yet there is so much to learn about the future from the beginning.

First, note that the LORD God personally planted it. This is presumably why it was called the Garden of God. It was not simply *spoken* into being as other things, but personally planted and crafted. If you have seen what wonderful gardens even we fallen, sinful, mortal creatures have planted then we can't imagine the utter wonders of this garden designed and planted by the eternal Son, expressing the Father's invisible glory in and through the creation.

It was filled with trees that were not only good for food but also pleasing to the eye. I love that! We tend to put more emphasis on function than form, yet in the garden of God the first priority is how pleasing it is to the eye. Given that He himself designed our eyes to view it, this garden must have been beyond all imagination.

Sometimes people worry that 'heaven' will be frightening because they imagine that it will be so utterly removed from human life. They fear that the life of the living God must be so utterly different from us that His environment will be terribly unpleasant. Yet if Eden is the garden that the LORD personally planted we can see that He created us with the same kind of taste as Himself and created a universe that reflects His own pleasure and purposes. We have been designed from the beginning to enjoy life in the creation with our God. The LORD that designed our eyes to be pleased by His creation will satisfy those eyes with sights of wonder and beauty.

Three heavens?

The Bible begins with the creation of the 'heavens' and the earth. We are told right away that there is more than one heaven. In fact Moses seems to describe three 'heavens'.

The **first** heaven is spoken of in Genesis 1:20 when the LORD creates birds to fly across the 'heaven'. These winged creatures, heavenly creatures of song according to Jesus Himself, have a lot to teach us. This first heaven is what we think of as the atmosphere, the expanse where the clouds float and the birds fly. Genesis 27:28 and Deuteronomy 33:13 speak of the 'dew from heaven' and Deuteronomy 11:11 and 28:12 both speak of the 'rain from heaven'.

So, if we think of the relationship between the heavens and the earth, in one sense we do in fact walk about in the heavens – from our feet up! We live each day in the forecourts of the heavens. We stand on the earth, but our heads are in the courts of heaven, in the first of the heavens. (This has much deeper significance than we can explore in this chapter, but we need only consider the profound significance of lifting a man up from the earth in his death).

Moses speaks of the **second** heaven in Genesis 1:17 as the place where all the stars are established. In Genesis 15:5 the LORD invites Abraham to count the stars of this second heaven as He explains just how numerous the church will become before the new creation begins. The second heaven is so glorious there is a danger we might try to worship the stars or even see them as controlling our lives here on earth. In Deuteronomy 4:19, the LORD says, 'And when you look up to the sky and see the sun, the moon and the stars – all the **heavenly** array – do not be enticed into bowing down to them.'

The first heaven is amazing, but how much greater and more incomprehensible is that second heaven. Many people are so mesmerised by the sheer size of the second heaven they are unable to even conceive of the highest heaven, the third heaven. One of the great tricks of science fiction is to project ultimate significance into this second heaven, imagining that all the answers to life on earth can be solved in a very big or very old universe possibly with 'sentient life' dotted around.

In pagan thought the size and grandeur of the second heaven seem to make people feel as if they have no meaning or significance at all. In the Bible, thinking of the vast wonders of the second heaven leads us to marvel at the importance of humanity in the plans of the Living God.

The third heaven – where the Father dwells

What of the third heaven that is even beyond the universe of stars and galaxies – this 'highest heaven' that Moses mentions in Deuteronomy 10:14? Look at Genesis 19:24:

> The LORD rained down burning sulphur on Sodom and Gomorrah – from the LORD out of the heavens.

The LORD on earth calls down burning sulphur from the LORD who is hidden in the heavens. In one sense, if we try the impossible and attempt to imagine the life of the Father, Son and Spirit as they existed before the universe existed, it is hard to understand how the Father might be in one place and the Son in another. In one sense they fill all the 'space': everything is relative to the Trinity, and they can be with us anywhere and everywhere.

Yet, before we limit the life of God into an abstract box, we need to remember that while the Father, Son and Spirit are beyond all spatial categories, yet at the same time the

Bible tells us about the place where the Father is enthroned and the fact that the Son sits next to Him.

If this doesn't blow the fuses of our minds, then nothing ever will!

Yes, all this cuts across the categories of philosophy, yet the Father has chosen the highest heaven as His special 'dwelling place'. The Father remains hidden on the other side of the wall of fire, the separating curtain, even though the Son and the Spirit have been sent to this side of the divide. The One God, whose life is fully and equally shared in the Father, Son and Spirit, engages with His creation in ways that seem incredible and impossible!

When the ancient church arrived in the Promised Land and set aside a tithe to pay for the Levites, widows and orphans, they were to pray to the Father in the highest heaven:

> 'I have obeyed the LORD my God; I have done everything you commanded me. Look down from heaven, **your holy dwelling place**, and bless your people Israel and the land you have given us as you promised.' (Deut. 26:14-15)

Too much glory for this earth!

When this hidden LORD joined heaven and earth in thick darkness at Sinai, with terrible thunder and lightning, His voice was too terrifying for the unbelieving people to hear:

> When the people saw the thunder and lightning and heard the trumpet and saw the mountain in smoke, they trembled with fear. They stayed at a distance and said to

Moses, 'Speak to us yourself and we will listen. But do not have God speak to us or we will die.' Moses said to the people, 'Do not be afraid. God has come to test you, so that the fear of God will be with you to keep you from sinning.' The people remained at a distance, while Moses approached the thick darkness where God was. Then the LORD said to Moses, 'Tell the Israelites this: "You have seen for yourselves that I have spoken to you from heaven".' (Exod. 20:18-22)

The majestic glory of the Father is simply too much for these heavens and earth as they are now. It is as if the earth is torn apart when the highest heaven is opened up with the Father's presence at Sinai. Moses trusts in the Angel of the LORD who has brought him to the Mountain of God – and so Moses is able to approach the glory and the thick darkness, but the unbelieving people want to stay at a distance.

The geographical barrier that separates the highest heaven and earth also exists in our own hearts and minds.

Who can bridge the gap?

The Angel of the LORD has a special role that takes Him to both the heavens and the earth. In fact, more than that, He is Himself the connection between the heavens and the earth.

In Genesis Jacob sees the LORD on or above a stairway reaching between the earth and the heavens. The created angels of God, carrying out their work throughout the whole heavens and the earth, are able to travel between the two, crossing the fiery barrier, passing through the curtain, only because of this ladder:

> Jacob left Beersheba and set out for Harran. When he reached a certain place, he stopped for the night because the sun had set. Taking one of the stones there, he put it under his head and lay down to sleep. He had a dream in which he saw a stairway resting on the earth, with its top reaching to heaven, and the angels of God were ascending and descending on it. There above it stood the LORD, and he said: 'I am the LORD, the God of your father Abraham and the God of Isaac. I will give you and your descendants the land on which you are lying. Your descendants will be like the dust of the earth, and you will spread out to the west and to the east, to the north and to the south. All peoples on earth will be blessed through you and your offspring. I am with you and will watch over you wherever you go, and I will bring you back to this land. I will not leave you until I have done what I have promised you.' When Jacob awoke from his sleep, he thought, 'Surely the LORD is in this place, and I was not aware of it.' He was afraid and said, 'How awesome is this place! This is none other than the house of God; this is the gate of heaven.' (Gen. 28:10-17)

The LORD stands above the stairway in heaven but also promises to be with Jacob on the earth. This 'gate of heaven' is none other than Jesus Himself, as He says in John 1:51.

The angel of the LORD, Jesus Christ, speaks from the third heaven to His people on earth. He is always the guarantee and the way of joining heaven and earth.

As Spurgeon says, Jesus enables all the business between heaven and earth, leading the angels in their ministry:

> The covenant Angel, the Lord Jesus, at the head of all the bands of heaven, surrounds with His army the dwellings of the saints. Like hosts entrenched so are the ministering spirits encamped around the Lord's chosen, to serve and succour, to defend and console them.[3]

The way back

The paradise of God, the mountain of the LORD, may seem so very far away in our exile. The way back seems to have been sealed so firmly that many of us have forgotten it altogether. With Jesus the gate of heaven is opened to us and we look forward to the heavens returning down to the earth.

There is obviously nothing we can do to make this happen. All attempts to break through the barrier to heaven in our own strength are not only forbidden but also impossible. In Genesis 11:1-9 the human race joined together to make their own way to heaven – 'Come, let us build ourselves a city, with a tower that reaches to the heavens, so that we may make a name for ourselves and not be scattered over the face of the whole earth.'

The LORD came down to the earth to judge and divide them!

The wall of fire, the separating curtain, can only be removed when the fundamental problem of sin is resolved. All other attempts only bring greater trouble and heartache.

---

3. *Treasury of David*, Psalm 34:7

So what can we do? What is Moses' advice as we live and die as exiles on earth?

> Now what I am commanding you today is not too difficult for you or beyond your reach. It is not up in heaven, so that you have to ask, 'Who will ascend into heaven to get it and proclaim it to us so we may obey it?' Nor is it beyond the sea, so that you have to ask, 'Who will cross the sea to get it and proclaim it to us so we may obey it?' No, the word is very near you; it is in your mouth and in your heart so you may obey it. (Deut. 30:11-14)

We don't need to find a way to break into heaven. We don't need to find a way to conquer death. Rather, the Word of the LORD God, Christ, is near to us, ready to be confessed and obeyed. Paul explains this passage of Deuteronomy in Romans 10:6-9:

> The righteousness that is by faith says: 'Do not say in your heart, "Who will ascend into heaven?" ' (that is, to bring Christ down) 'or "Who will descend into the deep?" ' (that is, to bring Christ up from the dead). But what does it say? 'The word is near you; it is in your mouth and in your heart,' that is, the message concerning faith that we proclaim: If you declare with your mouth, 'Jesus is Lord,' and believe in your heart that God raised him from the dead, you will be saved.

The heavens and the earth should not intimidate us, not even death itself, as long as we have Jesus.

When Moses considers all the heavens, even the highest heaven, he is driven to worship, love and faithful service:

24

'To the LORD your God belong the heavens, even the highest heavens, the earth and everything in it. Yet the LORD set his affection on your forefathers and loved them, and he chose you, their descendants, above all the nations, as it is today. Circumcise your hearts, therefore, and do not be stiff-necked any longer. For the LORD your God is God of gods and Lord of lords, the great God, mighty and awesome, who shows no partiality and accepts no bribes. He defends the cause of the fatherless and the widow, and loves the alien, giving him food and clothing. And you are to love those who are aliens, for you yourselves were aliens in Egypt.' (Deut. 10:14-19)

However glorious the second heaven may seem, with its nebula and stars, it is only the forecourt for the highest heaven, the third heaven, the place where the LORD God has established His throne. Yet, even that highest heaven has no glory compared to the uncreated glory and majesty of the Trinity. When we grasp this – the presence and glory of the Father through the Son in the fullness of the Spirit – then the vast mysteries of all the heavens are nothing compared to the God who cares for the weak and helpless.

As Rutherford reminded us at the beginning, it is the Lord Himself who is the true wonder and glory.

Going deeper still – the mountain of God

As we catch our breath, let's head back to the Garden of Eden. If we are going to understand more of the hope of heaven, we need to get a deeper understanding of paradise itself.

> A river watering the garden flowed from Eden; from there
> it was separated into four headwaters. (Gen. 2:10)

This extraordinary river flowed from Eden and, after it left Eden, split up into four other rivers that flowed out across the rest of the earth.

But what was the source of this master river that produced four such great rivers?

Rivers normally flow from mountains, yet what mountain could there be at the centre of Eden?

Throughout the Bible we hear of this mountain of God. We first hear of it in Exodus 3:1-2 – 'Moses was tending the flock of Jethro his father-in-law, the priest of Midian, and he led the flock to the far side of the desert and came to Horeb, the mountain of God. There the angel of the LORD appeared to him.'

In the next chapter Moses and Aaron meet at the mountain of God – Exodus 4:27. After the Exodus, Moses camps at the mountain of God – Exodus 18:5. Finally Moses and the church leaders are invited to come up the mountain of God to enjoy fellowship with Him:

> Moses and Aaron, Nadab and Abihu, and the seventy elders
> of Israel went up and saw the God of Israel. Under his feet
> was something like a pavement made of lapis lazuli, as bright
> blue as the sky. But God did not raise his hand against these
> leaders of the Israelites; they saw God, and they ate and drank.
> The LORD said to Moses, 'Come up to me on the mountain
> and stay here, and I will give you the tablets of stone with the
> law and commandments I have written for their instruction.'
> Then Moses set out with Joshua his aide, and Moses went up
> on the mountain of God. (Exod. 24:9-13)

It is as if the original mountain of God that was in Eden, the mountain of God that defines the centre of paradise, is given an earthly expression in Mount Sinai.

Mount Sinai becomes something like a **reminder** of that original and heavenly mountain that defines the paradise of God.

We might even say that the true mountain of God of the third heaven was in some way joined to the earthly Mount Sinai while the Law was given. For that time, there was some real link between the two.

Glory beyond imagination

Under the feet of the LORD 'was something like a pavement made of lapis lazuli, as bright blue as the sky'. This same bright, clear blue pavement or throne is noticed by others who are given a vision of the third heaven (see Ezekiel 1 and Revelation 4).

If you can imagine a vast expanse of lapis lazuli, then it looks like the whole universe, or the whole of the second heaven, stretched out under the feet of the LORD in the highest heaven. We could almost imagine that the floor of the highest heaven really **is** the second heaven with all its millions of galaxies and stars. That heavenly mountain of God is beyond all our philosophy and imagination.

Psalm 24 is all about the fact that none of us sinful people are able to ascend that true mountain of God. Only Jesus, the King of Glory, is able to ascend the mountain of God, returning from this exiled earth to the mountain paradise where the Father has established His throne.

Who may ascend the hill of the LORD?
Who may stand in his holy place?
He who has clean hands and a pure heart,
who does not lift up his soul to an idol
or swear by what is false.

(Ps. 24:3-4)

God's glory – filling the creation

Given that the book of Revelation mirrors the book of Genesis in so many ways, it is no surprise to read how the river of the water of life flows from the throne of the Father and the Son:

> Then the angel showed me the river of the water of life, as clear as crystal, flowing from the throne of God and of the Lamb down the middle of the great street of the city. On each side of the river stood the tree of life… (Rev. 22:1-2)

The point of all this is to give us a sense of the wonder and glory of the Garden of Eden. This was so much more than a National Trust garden! This was the place where the mountain of God joined with the earth, the source of the mighty water of life flowing out to the world.

Paradise is supposed to be the union of the heavens and the earth, the place where the glory of God flows out to His creation filling it with the ever-new beauty and purpose, life and order – that is His own eternal life.

In Ezekiel 28, we have another glimpse of this mount of God. The LORD has intense words of truth to tell to the spiritual ruler of Babylon:

> You were in Eden,
> the garden of God…
> You were anointed as a guardian cherub,
> for so I ordained you.
> You were on the holy mount of God;
> you walked among the fiery stones.
>
> (Ezek. 28:13-14)

Even Lucifer before he fell, walked across the universe, striding through the galaxies and the stars when the creation was newly made! Can we imagine a place of such wonder and glory? All this glory and wonder focused into the garden of God – here on planet earth.

True paradise!

Heaven and earth were joined together in this glorious garden. Instead of the 'curtain' that cuts us off from the mountain of God, in that garden there was a flow of life and communion between heaven and earth. The LORD Jesus walked in His garden, revelling in the whole creation with His bride, the special creatures that were copies of Him.

That is what we really mean by 'heaven'. Heaven is life in the presence of Jesus, to the glory of the Father, in the fullness of the Spirit. That is paradise.

The tabernacle – showing this great divide

One of the most fascinating parts of the whole Bible is the tabernacle. The LORD gave instructions to Moses about a tent-like structure to be constructed in the centre of the vast camp of wilderness refugees. This tent was a multi-media model of the whole of the heavens and the earth, with detailed activities of sacrifice, washings and festivals to explain how heaven and earth could be re-connected.

The instructions for the tabernacle recall the original state of the creation, when heaven and earth were still connected. We can think of the tabernacle as a building with two separated rooms, yet the LORD wanted His people to always think of it first as a single room with no division. The dividing curtain was only added as an 'extra' – it was not part of the fundamental structure of the tabernacle.

Remember that these instructions were given to Moses from heaven itself. The tabernacle was not a human piece of imagination but a model copied from heaven:

'Make this tabernacle and all its furnishings exactly like the pattern I will show you.' (Exod. 25:9)

In Acts, Stephen says that Moses was not simply told what to build but he *saw* the original pattern from which the tabernacle was copied:

'Our forefathers had the tabernacle of the Testimony with them in the desert. It had been made as God directed Moses, according to the pattern he had seen.' (Acts 7:44)

The writer to the Hebrews makes this even more explicit:

The point of what we are saying is this: We do have such a high priest, who sat down at the right hand of the throne of the Majesty in heaven, and who serves in the sanctuary, the true tabernacle set up by the Lord, not by man. Every high priest is appointed to offer both gifts and sacrifices, and so it was necessary for this one also to have something to offer. If he were on earth, he would not be a priest, for there are already men who offer the gifts prescribed by the law. They serve at **a sanctuary that is a copy and shadow of what is in heaven**. This is why Moses was warned when he was about to build the tabernacle: 'See to it that you make everything according to the pattern shown you on the mountain.' (Heb. 8:1-5)

Moses saw the structure of heaven itself! If we want to understand how the heavens and the earth are related together then here is our guide.

In Exodus 26:1-30 the tabernacle is described as one room, including the section that is later separated off as heaven. The curtain of separation, the very curtain that was torn down from top to bottom when Jesus died, **was only added in the next phase of the building process.**

When Adam and Eve refused to trust the LORD God and with Lucifer dragged the creation away from that glorious beginning, the wall of fire began – the separating curtain was put in place.

As soon as they stopped trusting Him that separation appeared within them. They wanted to get away from Him, hide from Him, even before the official division of heaven and earth.

The deep consequence of this lack of trust was not simply that Adam was divided within himself, but more seriously, 'the LORD God banished him from the Garden of Eden' (Gen. 3:23). Exile from the LORD's presence is at the heart of all this. This comes out explicitly when Cain heads away from

Eden into the east – 'Cain went out from the LORD's presence and lived in the land of Nod, east of Eden' (Gen. 4:16).

The exile from Eden, from paradise, was essentially the exile from the Father, Son and Holy Spirit. Where **they** are, the creation is at its most incredible and wonderful. Where the Trinity is, the creation is all that it can possibly be, both pleasing to the eye and good for purpose.

Where the Living God establishes His presence, there the creation is very good.

Eden is not 'it'

It is worth remembering that as glorious as it was, Eden wasn't the final and full destination for the universe.

Adam and Eve were told to subdue the whole earth, suggesting that there were parts of the creation **yet** to be brought into that incredible centre of unity between heaven and earth. There was still earth to subdue, to bring into the Garden of God.

Neither Adam nor Eve had seen the face of the Father, even though there was a special unity between heaven and earth. There was still night and darkness before each day, whereas in the final glorious new creation there will be no night.

In that original creation there was still the threat of death and evil, whereas after the day of resurrection there will be no more death and evil will never be heard from again.

We are not looking to simply return to Eden as it was at the beginning.

The hope that Christ set before Abraham and all the church since the beginning is of a city with foundations within that mountain garden and a renewal that reaches to every part of the creation.

However, we can see the great hope that is set before us in Jesus Christ.

We can in some ways glimpse the wonder and glory of the creation in those first days when the chaos and darkness, death and disease, sin and evil did not flood in.

Even now we can sense the groaning of creation both within ourselves and in the world around us, as the whole cosmos yearns to be delivered from this bondage of decay.

As we have tasted already the life of the age to come, we long to be on the other side of the wall of fire, with Abraham, Isaac and Jacob in the presence of Jesus.

But more than that we long for the time when the wall of separation will be gone completely and the whole creation, the heavens and the earth, will not just be restored to Eden, but taken on into the full maturity and perfection that was always planned from the very foundation of the world.

CHAPTER 2

OUTER DARKNESS

WE are used to thinking of judgement as something that comes at the end of the Bible. But at the very beginning the Father, through the Son, in the power of the Spirit **separated light from darkness**.

The Bible begins by telling us that God knows about good and evil. He determines what is good (as He does throughout the week of creation), and He alone determines the destiny and limits of darkness and chaos.

From day one He shows His complete mastery over them. They are powerless compared to His eternal light and order:

> In the beginning God created the heavens and the earth. Now the earth was formless and empty, darkness was over the surface of the deep, and the Spirit of God was hovering over the waters. And God said, 'Let there be light,' and there was light. God saw that the light was good, and he separated the light from the darkness. God called the light 'day', and

the darkness he called 'night'. And there was evening, and there was morning – the first day.[1] (Gen. 1:1-5)

Did God create the darkness?

It might be better to say that darkness is what happens when light isn't shining. Chaos is nothing. We can't find a bag full of 'chaos'. Chaos is what happens when things do not have order and structure.

Rather than imagine that the LORD created chaos, we see that He created the heavens and the earth in such a way that they had not yet received either the light or order of God the Word, the Eternal Son.

Without Jesus the heavens and the earth are lost in darkness and chaos.[2]

At the very beginning the cosmic light of Christ confronts the darkness and the darkness cannot resist, understand or overcome it – as John reminds us in John 1:1-5.

The story written into the universe

On the very first day God establishes the fact that darkness and chaos are powerless before His Word. The story of the universe is not an eternal equal battle between good and evil, but the victory march of light over darkness.

This is incredibly important. We all sense deep down that 'the great story' is the victory of good over evil. When we watch a film or read a book that takes us deep into that story

---

1. *The Holy Bible: New International Version*, 1996 (electronic ed.) (Gen. 1:1-5). Grand Rapids: Zondervan.

2. Jeremiah 4:22-29 spells this out in great and terrifying detail.

and lets us feel the drama of good triumphing over evil, we are moved so deeply.

The reason we feel these things is because this is the story that was written into the deepest fabric of the origin of the universe – more deeply than any of the so-called 'laws of nature'. Darkness does not take the living God by surprise. It is under His absolute rule and power from the start.

Adam and Eve tried to snatch the knowledge of good and evil for themselves, but that knowledge had already been established for ever by the Living God. We might think that evil and hell were only thought about after the sin of Adam, Eve and the devil, but the truth is that the LORD God had prepared for this long before.

He rules over the darkness

The word 'separate' is a key word in Genesis 1. Darkness is separated, divided from light.

God is light. He is the uncreated light of eternity. Darkness can only be seen or even conceived as the absence or rejection of Him. He creates darkness when He removes His light and blessing and presence, but darkness cannot create itself or even get a foothold against the light.

As we go through the Bible we see that He uses the darkness in His own judgements and work. Even when the darkness conceals things from us, yet to the LORD it is plain and open, unable to hide anything at all.

At the cross, when darkness seemed to be winning, the truth was that God was more powerful than ever and the light was shining more brightly than ever.

As we follow Jesus, in our own times of 'darkness' we need not despair or imagine that darkness is victorious. The mighty Spirit is working and we may know His presence and fruit as never before.

We may think that any mention of the darkness or chaos is entirely bad and it would be better if the universe had begun without ever even thinking of them. But the Bible takes a very different view. The separation of darkness and the defeat of chaos is a glorious manifestation of the majesty and wisdom of the Lord.

It gives great comfort and joy to know that darkness has already been given its place from the very foundation of the world.   .

Without Jesus creation unravels

> The earth was **formless and empty**, darkness was over the surface of **the deep**, and the Spirit of God was hovering over the waters. (Gen. 1:2)

There are three key words here. The first two, 'formless' and 'empty' are Hebrew words – *tohu* and *bohu*. Matthew Henry, the great Bible scholar of the early 18th century, says that whilst God could have made everything perfect from the very start, He allowed this time of chaos and darkness, this time of *tohu* and *bohu* because He wanted to teach us a great truth.

Think about the situation in Genesis 1:2. The heavens and the earth had been created, yet that Word by which all things are created, that Word that is the life and light of the cosmos, has not yet been revealed. He is there of course, sustaining all things, but He has not yet been revealed.

God wants to show us what the universe is like without Him.

Without Jesus the heavens and the earth are formless and empty. As soon as He is revealed and begins to shine in verse 3, the chaos retreats and the darkness is separated away.

In Jeremiah 4 the LORD warns His people that they do not know Him. They don't realise how utterly dangerous it is if they do not know Him. To be ignorant of Christ is not a merely 'religious' problem: it is a rejection of the very foundations and structure of the universe:

> 'My people are fools; they do not know me. They are senseless children; they have no understanding. They are skilled in doing evil; they know not how to do good.' I looked at the earth, and it was **formless** and **empty**; and at the heavens, and their light was gone. I looked at the mountains, and they were quaking; all the hills were swaying. I looked, and there were no people; every bird in the sky had flown away. I looked, and the fruitful land was a desert; all its towns lay in ruins before the LORD, before his fierce anger. (Jer. 4:22-26)

If there is no knowledge of the LORD then creation itself begins to unravel. If Christ is rejected there is no possible life.

He is the life of the heavens and the earth. He is the light of the universe. Without Him there simply is no light or life – no civilisation or order.

The Abyss – God's final judgement

The third word in Genesis 1:2 is translated with the English word 'deep'. This English word can mean several things in different contexts – a deep hole, a deep thought, a deep ocean, a deep cross in football or a deep darkness. But what about here? What is 'the deep' here in Genesis 1:2?

Some think that Moses is describing a situation where everything in the universe is mixed together in a chaotic **ocean** of material, where light and darkness, liquids and solids are all one meaningless mass. Then out of the random chaos God produces an ordered, separated universe.

This may well be a big part of the picture.

This word for 'deep' occurs several times throughout the Bible: the Hebrew word '*tehom*' or the Greek word '*abussos*'. This is where we get the English word 'abyss'.

There are times when the Hebrew word *tehom* can simply mean something like 'ocean' or even the 'depths of the earth'. At the end of the book of Genesis (49:25) Jacob gives a blessing that includes a reference to '*tehom*', referring simply to the depths of the ocean or the roots of the mountains.

But in other references it clearly has a deeper meaning with connections to the grave, to hell, to sorrow, to chaos and to darkness.

It is as if some of that ancient meaningless, chaotic 'ocean' is still left as a reminder outside or under the ordered creation.

The Abyss is much more than a restless ocean or the dark depths of the earth, but a more cosmic notion of chaos and darkness that is the very opposite of life and order.

In Luke 8:26-33 the demons beg Jesus not to send them into the Abyss. They know it is the very worst place.

To be thrown out away from Jesus is the ultimate judgement – into the outer darkness, away from His presence, into the bottomless pit where there is no foundation. To be thrown into the Abyss is to be thrown back into that deep, formless, empty darkness. If you are thrown out in this sense it is to be shut out from real life and light in the ultimate sense – as if your being is unravelled; as if everything that gives you substance is returned to Jesus and you are left falling forever, lost in chaotic darkness forever.

The language for deep waters and the Abyss run close together in the Bible. The restless salty ocean is a symbol of it. Think of the terrible inky black depths… no light, no air, no stability – no life as we know it.

In the Atlantic ocean there is a region called the Mariana Trench containing the very deepest parts of the ocean. The deep parts are called the Abyssal zone. The very bottom layer is called the Hadal zone – named after Hades itself. The demonic looking creatures inhabiting the depths are a vivid warning about the inhabitants of the Abyss. According to Job, Leviathan, the devil even swims in this Abyss (Job 41:32).

In Luke 8 the demons want to stay away from the Abyss, yet as soon as they go into the pigs, they race down the hill and into the sea, into the ocean. The Abyss calls to them. It is their true and final home. Cut off from Jesus, at war with the living God, there is no final place for them in the light and order of creation.

To be thrown into the Abyss is to have the LORD's final and ultimate 'No' spoken against you. It is to be shut out from all life and light and love and order and purpose.

The Abyss crops up many times in the book of Revelation (for example, 11:7, 17:8, 20:1, 3):

The fifth angel sounded his trumpet, and I saw a star that had fallen from the sky to the earth. The star was given the key to the shaft of the Abyss. When he opened the Abyss, smoke rose from it like the smoke from a gigantic furnace. The sun and sky were darkened by the smoke from the Abyss. (Rev. 9:1-2)

It is like a gigantic furnace. Only darkness and smoke come out of it.

It is like a bottomless lake of fire and darkness.

In Revelation we are told that even death and Hades are finally thrown into it.

Jesus refers to it as the 'outer darkness'.

It is 'outside' – it is shut out, excluded.

It is 'separated' – as we saw right at the beginning.

God's 'yes' and 'no'

In saying 'yes' to light and life and order, Jesus also says 'no' to chaos and darkness and death. Good and evil are defined before the world begins. From the very beginning the Living God shows that His purpose for the creation is not chaos.

When He made that deep division between light and darkness on day one, God was defining His 'yes' and His 'no' – showing us how utterly separated His 'yes' and 'no' are.

God divided the light from the darkness; they could never be joined together, or reconciled; for what fellowship has light with darkness? (2 Cor. 6:14).[3]

---

3. Henry, M. (1996). *Matthew Henry's commentary on the whole Bible: Complete and unabridged in one volume* (Gen. 1:3-5). Peabody: Hendrickson.

He gives light

Throughout the writings of Moses we see the ancient church enjoying light because of the presence of the LORD, whereas the enemies of the LORD are left in darkness:

> The LORD said to Moses, 'Stretch out your hand toward the sky so that darkness spreads over Egypt – darkness that can be felt.' So Moses stretched out his hand toward the sky, and total darkness covered all Egypt for three days. No one could see anyone else or move about for three days. Yet all the Israelites had light in the places where they lived. (Exod. 10:21-23)

> By day the LORD went ahead of them in a pillar of cloud to guide them on their way and by night in a pillar of fire to give them light, so that they could travel by day or night. Neither the pillar of cloud by day nor the pillar of fire by night left its place in front of the people. (Exod. 13:21-22)

In the presence of the LORD there is light and life and order. As we travel with Him to paradise, though we pass through times of darkness, barrenness and the shadow of death, if He is with us, we have His light to guide us.

Why night and day?

Surely we have a major question here. If it is true that God divided the light and the darkness so that they are forever in opposition, why did He create a cycle of evening then morning, night and day?

Why not have nothing but day in the earth from the very beginning? Why the state of fluctuation between darkness and light if the final purpose was to shut out the darkness forever?

Matthew Henry explains this very helpfully – if a little quaintly:

> God has thus divided time between light and darkness, because He would daily remind us that this is a world of mixtures and changes. In heaven there is perfect and perpetual light, and no darkness at all; in hell, utter darkness, and no gleam of light. In that world between these two there is a great gulf fixed; but, in this world, they are counterchanged, and we pass daily from one to another.[4]

God knew that the original state for the creation would not last long. He knew that the single biggest issue facing the world would be the choice between light and darkness, Christ and chaos. Every day He wanted to give us constant reminders that the darkness is defeated by the light; that the night is far spent and the morning is at hand; that the darkness can never comprehend the light; that evil behaviour happens in the darkness but the children of the light behave like God Himself.

Have we ever really understood what it is like to be without Jesus? We are speaking here of the deepest level of our being – about not knowing the One in whom we live and move. Even now, in the darkness, we may feel the waves of the Abyss lapping at our souls when we hide away from Him.

Think of the great evil done in the darkness. Think of the way that people behave at night-time, when the darkness

---

4. Ibid.

covers them. This is the condemnation – that we love darkness rather than light because our deeds are evil. Because of this we have felt the dark and chaotic waves of the Abyss in our hearts and minds, dragging us down into its inky depths.

That is what hell is all about.

That is why the Bible uses this word '*abussos*' to describe the only possible destiny for those who refuse Jesus.

Hell is not just something for the future, but even now we can experience the first touches of hell. Even now we experience the burning shame and the meaningless darkness and the gnawing emptiness if we try to exist away from Him.

Hell is bad because it is existence without Jesus the light, life and logic of the world.

That is why there is such wonderful and glorious news – 'God said, "Let there be light," and there was light. God saw that the light was good, and he separated the light from the darkness. God called the light "day", and the darkness he called "night". And there was evening, and there was morning – the first day.'

Paul writes, 'The god of this age has blinded the minds of unbelievers, so that they cannot see the light of the gospel of the glory of Christ, who is the image of God. For we do not preach ourselves, but Jesus Christ as Lord… For God, who said, "Let light shine out of darkness," made his light shine in our hearts to give us the light of the knowledge of the glory of God in the face of Christ.' (2 Cor. 4:6)

The most basic lesson in the universe

Have we learned the most basic lesson in the entire universe, the lesson written into the deepest fabric of the cosmos?

Have we responded to the good news that is preached to us every time the light is switched on, every time we see how easily darkness is defeated by light?

If we bow down before the LORD Jesus we do not need to fear the Abyss. We do not need to live in the darkness. We do not need to fall into that meaningless existence. We can be children of the light whose eternal destiny is not *tohu* and *bohu* but light and life and order and glory in that new creation future when there will no longer be any night at all.

When we look at the flood with Noah or the destruction of Sodom and Gomorrah or the Passover judgements in Egypt, the same fundamental truth is being played out. There is no life or light, health or safety once we are alienated from Christ.

Whether the judgement of death comes quickly in sudden destruction or more slowly through the course of a life, the destiny is unavoidable, fixed before the world began.

The consequences of sin, the fall into outer darkness, can be felt already in this life and show how the eternal destiny of sin is that *tohu* and *bohu* existence without Jesus.

Sin – and its consequences

In Genesis 4 Cain kills his brother. The LORD warns Cain about what is happening to him. Again we see how His life and order in creation is unravelled when we sin:

> The LORD said, 'What have you done? Listen! Your brother's blood cries out to me from the ground. Now you are under a curse and driven from the ground, which opened its mouth to receive your brother's blood from your hand. When you

work the ground, it will no longer yield its crops for you. You will be a restless wanderer on the earth.' Cain said to the LORD, 'My punishment is more than I can bear. Today you are driving me from the land, and I will be hidden from your presence; I will be a restless wanderer on the earth, and whoever finds me will kill me.' (Gen. 4:10-14)

Cain is cursed, rejected by the earth itself, forced to fight against the soil rather than work with it. Note how Cain describes his punishment: 'you are driving me from the land, and I will be hidden from **your** presence; I will be a restless wanderer on the earth.'

Because he is away from the LORD's presence, he is driven from the land and can find no rest on the earth. There is nothing left for him but a lost existence on earth and then that everlasting lost wandering of the outer darkness.

We can all see how sin brings such consequences, often in this life long before death and the final judgement.

Sin – turning away from God

There are four main Hebrew roots for 'sin'. The most common *ht* means deviating away or falling short. The next most frequent *pš* has the idea of rebellion or revolution. The third *wh* means a deliberate twisting or perversion. The fourth *šāḡâh* brings out the sense of going astray or error.[5]

Sin is deviation, rebellion, perversion and error. It is an attack on God and on His order of life and light in the heavens and the earth.

---

5. Wood, D. R. W., & Marshall, I. H. (1996). *New Bible Dictionary* (3rd ed.) (page 1105). Leicester, England; Downers Grove, Ill.: InterVarsity Press.

The **punishment** of sin is the logical extension of what sin **is**: death, darkness, chaos, emptiness, restlessness.

Hell is the natural home of sin, the logical destiny of sin, the expression of what sin really is.

No point remaining in this world

> The LORD saw how great the wickedness of the human race had become on the earth, and that every inclination of the thoughts of the human heart was only evil all the time. The LORD regretted that he had made human beings on the earth, and his heart was deeply troubled. So the LORD said, 'I will wipe from the face of the earth the human race I have created – and with them the animals, the birds and the creatures that move along the ground – for I regret that I have made them.' (Gen. 6:5-7)

The sinfulness not only corrupts the heart, producing terrible wickedness in human behaviour (and angelic too), but it is such a deep rejection or twisting of our created purpose that the LORD can see no point in our remaining in His world.

The punishment of sin is to be wiped off the face of the earth, to be thrown out with the rubbish, to be shut out into the outer darkness. If we rebel against the LORD who made us then how can we have a place in His world?

One of the problems with the folklore surrounding hell is that hell is portrayed as a very interesting and dynamic place – full of torture equipment and a vast demonic bureaucracy administering the anguish. It is seen as interesting and vibrant even if it is painful place of misery.

In the Bible hell is not like this. It is all that life is not. It is dark, lifeless and silent (Psalm 31:17). The only sound is the futile rage against the light. It is the very opposite of the life and light and order of the heavens and the earth. The LORD God's punishment for sin is to take the sinner away from the earth and throw him away into that outer darkness where there is only lifeless *existence*.

Glimpses of that final judgment – Noah

> In the six hundredth year of Noah's life, on the seventeenth day of the second month – on that day all the springs of **the great deep** burst forth, and the floodgates of the heavens were opened. And rain fell on the earth forty days and forty nights. (Gen. 7:11-12)

The story of the flood is especially powerful because the *tehom*, the deep, of Genesis 1:2 is mentioned again. That original 'deep' is allowed to overwhelm the world again. If the world rejects Jesus, then the punishment is to let it feel something of what that really means. The chaotic, restless 'deep' rolls back as the LORD removes His preserving power.

In the ark with the LORD, the light, life and order remain in a beautiful microcosm of the whole earth. Outside, the chaos and destruction are allowed to cover even the highest mountains.

When the judgement is over, when the wicked have been taken away from the earth, then the work of creation is re-established. Once again the LORD separates the sea from the dry land; once again the dry land produces vegetation.

God said to Noah, 'Come out of the ark, you and your wife and your sons and their wives. Bring out every kind of living creature that is with you – the birds, the animals, and all the creatures that move along the ground – so they can multiply on the earth and be fruitful and increase in number on it.'… Then Noah built an altar to the LORD and, taking some of all the clean animals and clean birds, he sacrificed burnt offerings on it. The LORD smelled the pleasing aroma and said in his heart: 'Never again will I curse the ground because of humans, even though every inclination of the human heart is evil from childhood. And never again will I destroy all living creatures, as I have done.' (Gen. 8:16-21)

The judgement brings about a kind of return to Eden. The old evil world is taken away and the new 'first family' hear again the instruction to 'be fruitful and multiply' as Adam and the animals heard in that very first week.

After Noah's burnt offering of atonement, the LORD renews His covenant with the earth. If He were to unravel creation because of the rebellion of the human heart He would have to destroy it over and over again.

The destruction of the whole world to make a true and final return to Eden will have to wait for the very end at the renewal of all things.

Sodom and Gomorrah

Just as Noah's flood is a sign of the final judgement through the Bible, so the destruction of Sodom and Gomorrah has the same significance. If the world was destroyed by the waters of 'the deep' in the flood, with Sodom destruction is by fire from heaven:

> By the time Lot reached Zoar, the sun had risen over
> the land. Then the LORD rained down burning sulphur
> on Sodom and Gomorrah – from the LORD out of the
> heavens. Thus He overthrew those cities and the entire
> plain, destroying all those living in the cities – and also
> the vegetation in the land. But Lot's wife looked back,
> and she became a pillar of salt. Early the next morning
> Abraham got up and returned to the place where he had
> stood before the LORD. He looked down toward Sodom
> and Gomorrah, toward all the land of the plain, and he
> saw dense smoke rising from the land, like smoke from a
> furnace. (Gen. 19:23-28)

The dividing wall of fire keeps us out of heaven. It can also be used against us, to drive us away and take us from the earth.

When we read about the behaviour of the men of Sodom we can see how far they had strayed from the life and logic of the LORD Jesus Christ. They not only thought it good to abuse angelic visitors, but they were outraged when Lot, even in his perverse and compromised way, suggested that they should not do it!

The judgement on Sodom, the falling of the fire from heaven, destroyed not only the evil people but also the cities and the vegetation. When Lot's wife yearned for that life she herself became a lifeless, barren block of salt. Abraham 'saw dense smoke rising from the land, like smoke from a furnace'.

This is truly a hellish scene. Life gone; the land ruined; the sun darkened; fire burning. It is no surprise that the rest of the Bible, and popular culture ever since, looks back to the destruction of Sodom and Gomorrah as one of the most vivid illustrations of the judgement of hell.

Pharaoh

Chapters 7-13 of Exodus take us through the character of hell and final judgement in the most detailed form anywhere in the whole Bible.

Pharaoh was a man who cared nothing for the LORD God of Israel. When given the initial command to let the ancient church go, he declared his position very clearly:

> Pharaoh said, 'Who is the LORD, that I should obey him and let Israel go? I do not know the LORD and I will not let Israel go.' (Exod. 5:2)

It is very unlikely that the Pharaoh was genuinely ignorant of the LORD God given that around 3 million of his slaves were all followers of Him. Yet, Pharaoh meant that this LORD had no place in his heart and mind. He cared nothing for Him.

The consequences of his attitude begin in chapter 5 with his mindless abuse of the LORD's people. Alienation from the LORD always moves quite quickly to alienation from other people. People sometimes imagine that hell will be like a wild party with all the wildest people. In fact all that we ever see of the destiny of sin, both now and in the age to come, is that there is nothing but loneliness and self-obsession.

The plagues

The plagues of judgement that come upon Egypt are not just arbitrary and random afflictions. Rather they all play out eternal issues. They reveal the real disease of sin.

When we looked at Eden we saw that at its centre was refreshing, living water. The first plague destroys water. The fertility and refreshment of the Nile turns into blood – a massive statement of death.

Next Pharaoh's rebellion brings about a flood of frogs. Not only were frogs unclean creatures according to the Law (Lev. 11:10) but Revelation 16:13 speaks of three demons that looked like frogs. Gnats and flies followed. It is no accident that the devil is referred to as Beelzebub: the lord of the flies. The whole land becomes unusable with these spiritually symbolic creatures. It is as if the devil and his armies are let loose to oppress Egypt.

When we are outside the presence of the LORD, the creation has no proper limits. The powers and principalities in the heavenly realms run amok. The animal world falls into chaos just as completely as human sinners.

Next the livestock perishes. Adam and Eve were given authority over the animals, but when we leave the presence of the LORD God the animal world gets dragged down too:

> Then the LORD said to Moses and Aaron, 'Take handfuls of soot from a furnace and have Moses toss it into the air in the presence of Pharaoh. It will become fine dust over the whole land of Egypt, and festering boils will break out on people and animals throughout the land.' So they took soot from a furnace and stood before Pharaoh. Moses tossed it into the air, and festering boils broke out on people and animals. (Exod. 9:8-10)

The destruction of Sodom looked like a furnace. Now soot from a furnace is thrown over the whole land, bringing out inner corruption in the form of festering boils. The rebellion that plagued the land and animals now settles on humanity as well. Hail hits the land, the animals and the people as the judgement begins to strike deeper.

The plague of locusts was particularly frightening – stripping away everything that was left. It rendered Egypt nothing but a barren, lifeless wilderness and the Egyptian officials realised the danger:

> Pharaoh's officials said to him, 'How long will this man be a snare to us? Let the people go, so that they may worship the LORD their God. Do you not yet realize that Egypt is ruined?' (Exod. 10:7)

The same Hebrew word describing the destruction of the flood and Sodom is used by the Egyptians as they see what Pharaoh's perverse rebellion has brought on them. All life, civilisation, light and order has been drained out of their world:

> They devoured all that was left after the hail – everything growing in the fields and the fruit on the trees. Nothing green remained on tree or plant in all the land of Egypt. (Exod. 10:15)

> Then the LORD said to Moses, 'Stretch out your hand toward the sky so that darkness spreads over Egypt – darkness that can be felt.' So Moses stretched out his hand toward the sky, and total darkness covered all Egypt for three days. No one could see anyone else or move about for three days. Yet all the Israelites had light in the places where they lived. (Exod. 10:21-23)

Egypt had become a terrible repeat of that cosmic deep darkness. In rejecting the Lord God, Egypt had fallen down into a formless, lifeless existence. Pharaoh's words at the end of Exodus 10 are deeply ominous:

> Pharaoh said to Moses, 'Get out of my sight! Make sure you do not appear before me again! The day you see my face you will die.' 'Just as you say,' Moses replied. 'I will never appear before you again.' (Exod. 10:28-29)

Pharaoh wanted no more chances. Moses, who was like God to Pharaoh, was rejected as firmly and deliberately as God Himself.

'Just as you say' – these are the terrible words that will sound out across hell itself on that final day.

In refusing to obey the gospel of Jesus, in embracing the darkness and chaos rather than light and life, every person who falls into hell will receive what they have already chosen for so long.

The final judgement of sin

In Exodus 11:4-6 the final harvest of sin is reached. In one sense, there is great mercy here. The sentence of death was for **every** person who stood with Pharaoh in his rebellion, yet the Lord limited the sentence of death to only the first-born males:

> At midnight the Lord struck down all the firstborn in Egypt, from the firstborn of Pharaoh, who sat on the throne, to the firstborn of the prisoner, who was in the dungeon, and the firstborn of all the livestock as well. Pharaoh and

all his officials and all the Egyptians got up during the night, and there was loud wailing in Egypt, for there was not a house without someone dead. (Exod. 12:29-30)

The judgement extended up to the gods of Egypt as well:

'On that same night I will pass through Egypt and strike down every firstborn of both people and animals, and I will bring judgment on all the gods of Egypt. I am the LORD.' (Exod. 12:12)

The final judgement on the last day will include the devil and all his armies. They too will be thrown out into that outer darkness, that barren, lonely chaos.

Moses has enabled us to see in basic and simple terms what the final destiny of sin and evil is really like. We can feel it now in this world when darkness and chaos, burning shame and gnawing regret grip us.

There may be many words to describe hell: the bottomless pit; the Abyss; the outer darkness; Gehenna; Abaddon; the lake of fire. Yet, when we follow the teaching of Moses we see what it is all about.

Everything that is good – every good and perfect gift – comes down from the Father of lights through His eternal Son, the divine Word, in the power of the Spirit. Everything to do with life and light, order and purpose, civilisation and creativity, logic and relationship… all these are from the overflowing life of Jesus in the Spirit.

When we are cut off from Him, even now, we fall inevitably and ultimately into death and darkness, chaos and emptiness, savagery and boredom, insanity and loneliness – outer darkness.

CHAPTER 3

JUDGEMENT AND DEATH

WE have seen how there can be no lasting place for unbelief or sin in the world. Sooner or later the LORD God will drive out everything opposed to Him. Everyone who stands against Him will be destroyed and cast into outer darkness.

What divides heaven and hell is the presence of the LORD Himself.

In Leviticus 10 we see this powerfully in the story of Nadab and Abihu:

> Aaron's sons Nadab and Abihu took their censers, put fire in them and added incense; and they offered unauthorized fire before the LORD, contrary to his command. So fire came out from the presence of the LORD and consumed them, and they died before the LORD. Moses then said to Aaron, 'This is what the LORD spoke of when he said: "Among those who approach me I will be proved holy; in the sight of all the people I will be honoured".' Aaron remained silent. Moses

summoned Mishael and Elzaphan, sons of Aaron's uncle Uzziel, and said to them, 'Come here; carry your cousins outside the camp, away from the front of the sanctuary.' So they came and carried them, still in their tunics, outside the camp, as Moses ordered. Then Moses said to Aaron and his sons Eleazar and Ithamar, 'Do not let your hair become unkempt and do not tear your clothes, or you will die and the LORD will be angry with the whole community. But your relatives, all the Israelites, may mourn for those the LORD has destroyed by fire. Do not leave the entrance to the tent of meeting or you will die, because the LORD's anointing oil is on you.' So they did as Moses said. (Lev. 10:1-7)

We need not concern ourselves right now with the precise offence committed by Nadab and Abihu, but we do need to understand what happened in terms of the reality of death and separation.

One day we will view judgement as Jesus does

Aaron's own sons were destroyed by the consuming fire and yet as the anointed high priest, the one representing the LORD Himself, Aaron could show no sympathy or grief for them.

This is hard to grasp. Aaron has to side with the LORD against his own sons who had defiled the holiness of the LORD.

It has struck me more and more over the years as I have read the Bible how Jesus Himself speaks about hell and the day of judgement. We may get very stressed even if we were going to sack somebody from a job. The thought of sending someone out into the eternal darkness is beyond us. We tend to be very squeamish about sending anybody to hell, so much so that some of us simply run away from the idea of hell.

However, Jesus, who speaks about it more than anybody else, is the very person who will pass this eternal verdict on countless millions. In all His teaching **He** is the one who shuts people out and throws them into the lake of fire. His love for the world is unquestioned and yet He is not at all hesitant about doing this. There is no uncertainty or reluctance to perform this final act of judgement.

As the great high priest and judge, Jesus is not full of anxiety over the judgement that He brings.

We need to think about this.

We will side with the LORD against all those who have rejected Him, and that may include our family and friends.

We may find this too hard to deal with right now, but it is important to know when we are so completely taken up with the LORD Himself on that glorious day of resurrection, when the highest heaven comes down to the earth, we will view the wicked as He does.

To be exposed to Him would mean our destruction

Notice how fire came out from the presence of the LORD, confronting and destroying Nadab and Abihu.

The fire that guards the division between heaven and earth has this active dimension. We may think of the cosmic curtain between heaven and earth as a passive barrier that simply hangs there. But in the Bible the fire that surrounds the living God is dangerous. Those that defy or defile that curtain between the heavens and earth are in grave danger of being destroyed by it.

In the tabernacle the dividing curtain was made of blue, purple and scarlet thread (Exod. 26:31), a tapestry of fire and angelic guardians. This holy fire is a terrible danger to sinful humanity.

What is it there for? Who is being protected? Who is being shielded? The division between heaven and earth does not so much protect the Living God from us (as if He needed any protection!) but us from Him.

The LORD Jesus is the source of infinite life and light. Once we have been cut off from Him, if we are exposed to His full divine glory we will quickly be destroyed.

We need to return into His presence, but if we try to enter without being first forgiven and cleansed we are destroyed by that very presence.

Hell is so often characterised by fire because it is so completely and utterly shut out from the LORD's presence. For us to enter into the highest heaven, for the Father to ever come down to dwell with us, this consuming fire must be dealt with.

Remember the words spoken by the Father from the thick darkness of Sinai when the people had been worshipping the golden calf:

> '…I will not go with you, because you are a stiff-necked people and I might destroy you on the way.' When the people heard these distressing words, they began to mourn and no one put on any ornaments. For the LORD had said to Moses, 'Tell the Israelites, "You are a stiff-necked people.

**If I were to go with you even for a moment, I might
destroy you**…"' (Exod. 33:3-5)

He cannot be with them for even a moment without destroying them. They are so polluted by sin and death that the presence of His purity and life will consume them.

The living God is dangerous!

This truth is first brought out in Exodus 19 when they arrive at Mount Sinai. The whole point of the Exodus had been to come to worship in the presence of the LORD God, and yet the prospect of this encounter is fraught with danger. The presence of the LORD is simply not safe for sinful people.

He is not a 'household god' (Gen. 31:19, 34) sitting quietly in the corner! He is far more terrible and fearsome than that. His presence is dangerous. He cannot contain this consuming fire if people wander into His presence without His own preparation and protection:

> On the morning of the third day there was thunder and lightning, with a thick cloud over the mountain, and a very loud trumpet blast. Everyone in the camp trembled. Then Moses led the people out of the camp to meet with God, and they stood at the foot of the mountain. Mount Sinai was covered with smoke, because the LORD descended on it in fire. The smoke billowed up from it like smoke from a furnace, and the whole mountain trembled violently. As the sound of the trumpet grew louder and louder, Moses spoke and the Voice of God answered him. The LORD descended to the top of Mount Sinai and called Moses to the top of the mountain. So Moses went up and the LORD

said to him, 'Go down and warn the people so they do not force their way through to see the Lord and many of them perish. Even the priests, who approach the Lord, must consecrate themselves, or **the Lord will break out against them**.' Moses said to the Lord, 'The people cannot come up Mount Sinai, because you yourself warned us, "Put limits around the mountain and set it apart as holy".' The Lord replied, 'Go down and bring Aaron up with you. But the priests and the people must not force their way through to come up to the Lord, or **he will break out against them**.' (Exod. 19:16-24)

He simply cannot restrain His glory and majesty, His life and power, if a sinful, dying creature attempts to force his way through.

When it was extremely cold last winter my hands had become so devoid of warmth they were like blocks of ice. They needed warmth, but when I tried to wash them in warm water it was just too much and I couldn't handle it. The warmth that they lacked was too much to bear because they had become so cold.

Whether this analogy works I'm not sure, but it is as if we have become so alienated from the life of God that the very life that we desperately need will destroy us. To touch at eternal life again, without first being forgiven and cleansed, destroys us.

Passive punishment of sin

Remember Genesis 2: 'for when you eat from it you will certainly die' (v. 17)? The certain death that comes from our sinning is a deep truth with many aspects to it. Our death is certain once we are cut off from the life of Jesus.

There are perhaps two aspects to this punishment of sin. On the one hand there is a passive judgement and on the other an active one.

On the one hand the withdrawal of the LORD's presence means the withdrawal of His light, life and logic. To simply be pushed away from the LORD's presence means a withering and dying in the darkness. To be cut off from Him means that a person is cut off from light and life. Once a flower has been cut, no matter how fresh and vibrant it may seem for the next day or two, yet it is certainly dying and it is just a matter of time before it becomes a dry, shrivelled ruin.

We can call this the passive punishment of sin.

We can see how the final punishment of hell has aspects of this. To be shut out of the new creation or thrown into the bottomless Abyss means a complete and never-ending alienation from the life and light of Jesus. There is no way to find any comfort or forgiveness or fellowship in that outer darkness.

Active punishment of sin

On the other hand there is a much more active punishment that brings that inevitable death and destruction right to the moment. This is what we saw at the beginning of the chapter with Nadab and Abihu. It is what the Day of Judgement is all about when the LORD Jesus will descend in great glory to actively bring consuming fire against the world and everything in it.

There are occasions in the Bible when the LORD actively brings that destiny forward as He destroys those who stand against Him.

Look at this incident in Numbers 11:1-3:

> Now the people complained about their hardships in the hearing of the LORD, and when he heard them his anger was aroused. Then fire from the LORD burned among them and consumed some of the outskirts of the camp. When the people cried out to Moses, he prayed to the LORD and the fire died down. So that place was called Taberah,[1] because fire from the LORD had burned among them.

But nowhere does this come out so starkly as in the case of Korah's rebellion.

Creation joins with its maker to judge rebels

> Then Moses said, 'This is how you will know that the LORD has sent me to do all these things and that it was not my idea: If these men die a natural death and suffer the fate of all mankind, then the LORD has not sent me. But if the LORD brings about something totally new, and the earth opens its mouth and swallows them, with everything that belongs to them, and **they go down alive into the realm of the dead**, then you will know that these men have treated the LORD with contempt.' As soon as he finished saying all this, the ground under them split apart and the earth opened its mouth and swallowed them and their

---

1. Hebrew for 'burning'.

households, and all those associated with Korah, together with their possessions. **They went down alive into the realm of the dead, with everything they owned; the earth closed over them, and they perished and were gone from the community**. At their cries, all the Israelites around them fled, shouting, 'The earth is going to swallow us too!' And fire came out from the LORD and consumed the 250 men who were offering the incense. The LORD said to Moses, 'Tell Eleazar son of Aaron, the priest, to remove the censers from the charred remains and scatter the coals some distance away, for the censers are holy – the censers of the men who sinned at the cost of their lives...' (Num. 16:28-38)

Not only does the earth open to swallow Korah and his associates but fire comes out from the LORD and consumes 250 people. Can we imagine what this looked like, as the earth itself came alive to swallow these people?

Creation itself joined with its maker in judging the rebels.

The Hebrew says that Korah and his followers were taken down to **Sheol** with all they possessed. As Jesus symbolically went up at His ascension, indicating that He was going to the highest heaven, so these people were symbolically swallowed up by the earth, indicating that they were taken down, under the earth, to death and Hades.

Their death and judgement were brought right into the present moment and executed with decisive and terrifying power. Even the charred remains of those burnt with the LORD's holy fire had to be treated as unclean and the holy censers had to be retrieved from the smoking bodies.

It is so easy to create a domesticated version of God in our minds and hearts – treating Him like a pet cat rather than a terrifying lion. This LORD God of Israel loves with such great passion and He will go to any lengths to redeem His people – yet to those who will not have Him, who defy Him to the face, there is a fiery judgement and a terrible eviction to come.

Again and again we see that there can be no place in the presence of the LORD for those who sin against Him; for those who defy Him; for those who are cut off from Him in their selfishness and darkness.

Whether in sudden active judgement or through the slower, but just as certain, more passive judgement of exile and alienation, the sinner will surely die and be cast out of the world of life and light into the chaos and darkness of the Abyss.

The plague – a symptom of this present darkness

After Korah's judgement there is a plague:

> …the LORD said to Moses, 'Get away from this assembly so I can put an end to them at once.' And they fell face down. Then Moses said to Aaron, 'Take your censer and put incense in it, along with burning coals from the altar, and hurry to the assembly to make atonement for them. **Wrath has come out from the LORD; the plague has started**.' So Aaron did as Moses said, and ran into the midst of the assembly. The plague had already started among the people, but Aaron offered the incense and made atonement for

them. He stood between the living and the dead, and the plague stopped. But **14,700 people died from the plague, in addition to those who had died because of Korah**. Then Aaron returned to Moses at the entrance to the tent of meeting, for the plague had stopped. (Num. 16:44-50)

The anger of God against sin and evil is no pretence. It is clear that He wants to get rid of these people who have provoked Him to His face. His desire to cast them all away into outer darkness is very real.

When He restrains His anger or deals with that righteous indignation in some other way, it is an incredible miracle. His anger is justified and proportionate and righteous and controlled.

It is taken very seriously by Moses and Aaron, so we need to be equally serious about it today.

The effect of this anger going out from the LORD is a terrible plague spreading through the camp.

Death, disease, decay and depression are all ultimately symptoms of living in this present darkness, this passing age, this time of exile and alienation from God. These aspects of our mortal life are symbolically sent outside the camp in the book of Leviticus. When we live in the glorious, unrestricted presence of the LORD, in our heavenly, new creation future there will be no disease, no death, no depression, no decay.

One standing at the boundary

The plague was only stopped when the high priest stood in the path of the plague, making atonement. 14,700 died before it could be stopped and it was only stopped by atonement. God's wrath would have taken everyone away in mere moments, unless it was 'satisfied' on the boundary of the living and the dead.

This is deep truth. In our whole thinking about heaven and hell, it has become clear that the One who stands at the boundary between the two, the One who actually defines the boundary between the two, the One who sets the boundary between light and darkness, heaven and hell, is the LORD Jesus, the Great High Priest.

If we come to Him then we find in Him light and life, order and purpose, logic and sanity flowing away into His everlasting future of a renewed heavens and earth. If we turn from Him then we fall away into darkness and death, chaos and emptiness.

Jesus as the dividing point between life and death, heaven and hell, is brought out in a striking way in *The Last Battle* by C. S. Lewis:

> The creatures came rushing on, their eyes brighter and brighter as they drew nearer and nearer to the standing Stars. But as they came right up to Aslan one or the other of two things happened to each of them. They all looked straight in his face, I don't think they had any choice about that. And when some looked, the expression of their faces changed terribly – it was fear and hatred… And all the creatures who looked at Aslan in that way swerved to their right, his left, and disappeared into his huge black shadow which… streamed away to the left of the doorway. The children never saw them again. I don't know what became of them.

But the others looked in the face of Aslan and loved him, though some of them were very frightened at the same time. And all these came in at the Door, in on Aslan's right. There were some queer specimens among them. Eustace even recognized one of those very Dwarfs who had helped to shoot the Horses. But he had not time to wonder about that sort of thing (and anyway it was no business of his) for a great joy put everything else out of his head.[2]

Clean and unclean

This matter of coming into the gathering around Jesus, into the light and life, as opposed to being shut outside in the death and darkness, comes out very strongly in the Levitical teaching about the clean and the unclean.

Leviticus divides everything up into basically three categories: the holy, the common/clean and the unclean.

The *holy things* were those things exclusively dedicated to the LORD Himself – the priests, the tabernacle, and the equipment used at the tabernacle.

The *clean or common things* were all acceptable within the camp (the church community). The clean or common could approach into the presence of the LORD without harm.

The *unclean* were the people or things that had become polluted by the taint of sin or the consequences of this sinful world. Death, disease, decay, blood loss and deformity all could exclude a person from the presence of God. To even touch death or disease made a person unclean. All that was unclean had to be taken outside the camp. Beyond them, in the wilderness, was the place of the demons.

---

2. C. S. Lewis, 'The Last Battle', Harper Collins, New York, 2002, p. 170.

The diseased person who was outside the camp was not condemned to hell, but he had to bear witness to the problem of sin, death and disease. By staying outside the camp he was preaching the fact that in the LORD's presence there is no death, disease, deformity or uncleanness. One day the divine High Priest would bring them into God's presence and deliver them from all these problems.

In the LORD's presence, in paradise, in heaven, in the new creation, there is no death, no disease, no deformity, no uncleanness, no decay. Away from Him, in that outer place of exclusion, there is only death, disease, decay and uncleanness.

All these evils are finally thrown into the bottomless Abyss, along with all those who love the darkness rather than the light of Jesus.

What about the death of the righteous?

What happens to the righteous when they die? Do they have to wait until the day of resurrection to receive life in Jesus or do they get that straight away?

In Numbers there is a remarkable verse, spoken by the strange and greedy prophet Balaam (Num. 23:10 KJV) – 'Let me die the death of the righteous, and let my last end be like his.' What a marvellous verse! The greatest achievement of life is to die as a righteous person.

So far we have got a general understanding of heaven and hell from the Pentateuch. We have been looking at the fundamental character of the community of Jesus as opposed to the fragmented, chaotic darkness of those who reject Him. We have seen how the destiny of the righteous is to enjoy the united heavens and earth, as paradise, in the presence of the Father, Son and Spirit forever and ever. We have also seen how the destiny of the unrighteous is to be shut out from life, light, order and community forever and ever. It is the difference between light and darkness, order and chaos, life and death.

But what about while we wait? What about when we die?

Sheol – into the ground for burial and decay

We noticed earlier how Korah and his followers were swallowed alive by the earth and taken down into Sheol. Perhaps we need to take a moment to consider what Sheol might be. There are only seven direct references to Sheol in the Pentateuch (Gen. 37:35; 42:38; 44:29, 31; Num. 16:31, 33 and Deut. 32:22). Each of these references is very negative and most of them come from Jacob when he is wallowing in depression and grief over Joseph:

> Jacob tore his clothes, put on sackcloth and mourned for his son many days. All his sons and daughters came to comfort him, but he refused to be comforted. 'No,' he said, 'I will continue to mourn until I join my son in the grave (Sheol).' So his father wept for him. (Gen. 37:34-35)

> Jacob said, 'My son will not go down there with you; his brother is dead and he is the only one left. If harm comes to him on the journey you are taking, you will bring my gray head down to the grave (Sheol) in sorrow.' (Gen. 42:38)

We know that Jacob will be in the new creation on resurrection morning. If we take the words of Jesus at face value in Mark

12:26-27 then Jacob lives in the presence of God right now. Therefore Bible translators have used the word 'grave' to translate the Hebrew word 'Sheol' when Jacob speaks, as if Jacob were simply saying 'I'm going to live in sorrow until the day I die; until the day you bury me in the ground.'

If Sheol means nothing more than 'buried in the ground when I die', then every living creature goes to Sheol, into the ground for burial and decay. However, when we go further into the Bible we see that it means much more than 'burial' and Jacob's words need deeper thought.

When Jacob felt completely overwhelmed with grief and could see no hope in his life at all, he felt as if he were doomed to Sheol. Jacob had got so low that he felt as if he wasn't saved, that he was lost, that the LORD had forgotten him. Even strong and mature Christians can fall into this kind of gloom if the circumstances of life overwhelm them or when their thoughts are taken captive by the world rather than by Christ. Many of us know what it is to feel that we are lost, that we have lost our assurance. When we read the words of grieving Jacob we should read them with compassion and empathy if we want to understand their meaning.

Sheol – the realm of the dead

In the other three references to Sheol the translators go for a much more negative and metaphysical phrase – 'the realm of the dead':[3]

---

3. The Baker Evangelical Dictionary has the following description:
   Through much of the Old Testament period, it was believed that all went one place, whether human or animal whether righteous or wicked. No one could avoid Sheol which was thought to be down in the lowest parts of the earth.
   Unlike this world, Sheol is devoid of love, hate, envy, work, thought,

'if the LORD brings about something totally new, and the earth opens its mouth and swallows them, with everything that belongs to them, and they go down alive into the realm of the dead (Sheol), then you will know that these men have treated the LORD with contempt.' As soon as he finished saying all this, the ground under them split apart and the earth opened its mouth and swallowed them and their households, and all those associated with Korah, together with their possessions. They went down alive into the realm of the dead (Sheol), with everything they owned; the earth closed over them, and they perished and were gone from the community. (Num. 16:30-33)

The LORD says, 'a fire will be kindled by my wrath, one that burns down to the realm of the dead below (Sheol). It will devour the earth and its harvests and set afire the foundations of the mountains.' (Deut. 32:22)

The third reference to Sheol comes in Psalm 49, which was written by the sons of Korah. This is of great significance because those boys witnessed their own father falling down into Sheol.[4]

The story of Korah leaves a deep impact on us today. Imagine witnessing what happened that day. Imagine if Korah was your father and you had been forced to make the terrible choice between him and the LORD. That is the sort

---

knowledge, and wisdom. Descriptions are bleak: There is no light, no remembrance, no praise of God, in fact, no sound at all. Its inhabitants are weak, trembling shades who can never hope to escape from its gates. Sheol is like a ravenous beast that swallows the living without being sated.

4. 'Even if these "sons of Korah" are the distant descendants of the original sons, the concern for salvation from Sheol seems to have stuck with the family line.'

of experience that would shape the rest of your life – and it did for those sons!

Psalm 49
Of the Sons of Korah. A psalm.

Why should I fear when evil days come, when wicked deceivers surround me – those who trust in their wealth and boast of their great riches?

No man can redeem the life of another or give to God a ransom for him – the ransom for a life is costly, no payment is ever enough – that he should live on forever and not see decay.

For all can see that wise men die; the foolish and the senseless alike perish and leave their wealth to others. Their tombs will remain their houses forever, their dwellings for endless generations, though they had named lands after themselves. But man, despite his riches, does not endure; he is like the beasts that perish. This is the fate of those who trust in themselves, and of their followers, who approve their sayings. *Selah*

Like sheep they are destined for the grave (Sheol), and death will feed on them. The upright will rule over them in the morning; their forms will decay in the grave (Sheol), far from their princely mansions. But **God will redeem my life from the grave (Sheol); he will surely take me to himself**. *Selah*

Do not be overawed when a man grows rich, when the splendour of his house increases; for he will take nothing with him when he dies, his splendour will not descend with him. Though while he lived he counted himself blessed – and men praise you when you prosper – he will join the generation of his fathers, who will never see the light (of life). A man who has riches without understanding is like the beasts that perish. (Ps. 49:5-20)

We leave it all behind

The sons of Korah had seen very vividly when their father was taken down to Sheol with all his possessions, that the rich man 'will take nothing with him when he dies, his splendour will not descend with him'. Whatever wealth we might grasp together in this mortal life has no currency at all in Sheol, in the grave.

Nothing we can do in this life, no amount of money or achievements, can ever save us from death. We must all die. 'All can see that wise men die; the foolish and the senseless alike perish.' Rather than put death entirely out of our minds as if it were something avoidable, we must face it properly and be ready for it.

No light of life

Sheol is the very opposite of life and light. It is the opposite of the presence of the LORD. There is no light of life in Sheol. Psalm 88, also by the sons of Korah, describes being abandoned to Sheol:

> For my soul is full of trouble and my life draws near the grave.
> I am counted among those who go down to the pit;
> I am like a man without strength.

I am set apart with the dead, like the slain who lie in the
grave,
whom you remember no more, who are cut off from your
care.
You have put me in the lowest pit, in the darkest depths.
Your wrath lies heavily upon me; you have overwhelmed
me with all your waves. *Selah*
You have taken from me my closest friends and have made
me repulsive to them. I am confined and cannot escape;
my eyes are dim with grief.
I call to you, O LORD, every day; I spread out my hands
to you.
Do you show your wonders to the dead? Do those who are
dead rise up and praise you? *Selah*
Is your love declared in the grave, your faithfulness in
Abaddon?
Are your wonders known in the place of darkness, or your
righteous deeds in the land of oblivion?

(Ps. 88:3-12)

Those in Sheol have no strength They are forgotten by the
LORD and He does not care for them. His anger lies on them.
In that dark oblivion they have no friends, no escape, no
praise of the LORD, no awareness of His love or faithfulness,
no knowledge of the LORD.

The man who trusts in himself or in his riches will die
like a sheep, like a beast. He is abandoned into Sheol without
any hope. 'Though while he lived he counted himself blessed
– and men praise you when you prosper – he will join the
generation of his fathers, who will never see the light (of life).'

Redeemed from the grave

Although it may seem that Sheol has the last word and keeps everybody locked up in the grave or the realm of the dead – those who trust in the LORD, who are citizens of the city of God, are not held by Sheol:

> God will redeem my life from the grave (Sheol); he will surely take me to himself.

What does it mean that God will take me to Himself – away from Sheol? If we go to the previous sequence of psalms, again all by the sons of Korah, we might get more of an idea. Remember, that the sons of Korah were living at the time of Moses and Joshua, long before David had built the city of Jerusalem. When these psalms talk about the 'city of God' there is no city of Jerusalem for them to think about! They were thinking of another city and another mountain entirely, one whose builder and maker is the living God.

Psalm 45, the Messiah's wedding psalm, speaks of His throne lasting forever. There is a kingdom beyond the kingdoms of this world:

> Your throne, O God, will last for ever and ever; a sceptre of justice will be the sceptre of your kingdom. You love righteousness and hate wickedness; therefore God, your God, has set you above your companions by anointing you with the oil of joy. (Ps. 45:6-7)

The great city of God

> God is our refuge and strength, an ever-present help in trouble. Therefore we will not fear, though the earth give

way and the mountains fall into the heart of the sea, though its waters roar and foam and the mountains quake with their surging. *Selah*

There is a river whose streams make glad the city of God, the holy place where the Most High dwells. God is within her, she will not fall; God will help her at break of day. Nations are in uproar, kingdoms fall; He lifts his voice, the earth melts. The Lord Almighty is with us; the God of Jacob is our fortress. (Ps. 46:1-7)

Remember what we learned about paradise from the first chapter. Paradise is defined by a glorious mountain where a river of living water flows out. Now we are reminded of the great city of God on that glorious mountain. The centre piece of this great city is the holy place where the Most High, God the Father Himself, dwells.

The ascended Christ takes His throne

The next psalm, is full of exuberant joy. It is a psalm looking to the ascension of the LORD Jesus, when He ascends up to the city of God and takes His eternal throne:

God has ascended amid shouts of joy, the Lord amid the sounding of trumpets. Sing praises to God, sing praises; sing praises to our King, sing praises. For God is the King of all the earth; sing to him a psalm of praise. (Ps. 47:5-7)

The heavenly city

Finally Psalm 48 brings these psalms to an incredible end with a mind-blowing vision of this heavenly city of the living God:

> Great is the LORD, and most worthy of praise, in the
> city of our God, his holy mountain. It is beautiful in
> its loftiness, the joy of the whole earth. Like the utmost
> heights of Zaphon is Mount Zion, the city of the Great
> King. God is in her citadels; He has shown himself to be
> her fortress… Walk about Zion, go around her, count her
> towers, consider well her ramparts, view her citadels, that
> you may tell of them to the next generation. For this God
> is our God for ever and ever; he will be our guide even to
> the end. (Ps. 48:1-3; 12-14)

Korah's sons had fixed their hearts and minds on the city of
God, on His holy mountain. They were looking upwards to
their ascended God, to His everlasting throne and lofty city,
the city of the great king. They thought about the dwelling
of the LORD and they knew that when they died He would
not let them fall into Sheol but would take them to be with
Himself.

The city of God is a constant theme of their psalms. After
the terrible events of Numbers 16, they were passionate about
the alternative.

Born in Zion!

In this life, our riches count for nothing and neither does
our national or cultural background. Nothing matters more
than being a citizen of the city of God, a person named in
His register, a child known to the LORD.

Look at another psalm of the sons of Korah:

> He has set his foundation on the holy mountain; the
>   LORD loves the gates of Zion more than all the

79

dwellings of Jacob. Glorious things are said of you,
O city of God: *Selah*

'I will record Rahab and Babylon among those who
acknowledge me –

Philistia too, and Tyre, along with Cush – and will say,
"This one was born in Zion".'

Indeed, of Zion it will be said, 'This one and that one were
born in her, and the Most High himself will establish
her.' The LORD will write in the register of the peoples:
'This one was born in Zion.' *Selah*

As they make music they will sing, 'All my fountains are
in you.'   (Ps. 87)

The sons of Korah had such clear hope as they faced death –
the city of the living God. To be born in Zion, regardless of
our natural birth, is the basis of all our hope and joy.

How lovely is your dwelling place,
O LORD Almighty!
My soul yearns, even faints,
for the courts of the LORD;
my heart and my flesh cry out
for the living God.

Even the sparrow has found a home,
and the swallow a nest for herself,
where she may have her young –
a place near your altar,
O LORD Almighty, my King and my God.
Blessed are those who dwell in your house;
they are ever praising you. *Selah*

Look upon our shield, O God;
look with favour on your Christ.

Better is one day in your courts
than a thousand elsewhere;
I would rather be a doorkeeper in the house of my God
than dwell in the tents of the wicked.
For the LORD God is a sun and shield.

(Ps. 84:1-4; 9-11)

CHAPTER 4

RESURRECTION AND THE RENEWAL OF THE UNIVERSE

MANY people claim to believe in heaven and hell, but what do their lives teach? Our beliefs are always shown in the way we live rather than the words we speak.

Moses liked to teach doctrine in action. When we read Moses we have to look at how the people lived and the events that happened to them if we are to grasp the truth that is being taught.

When we read about Abraham we can clearly see his resurrection hope by the way he lived. Lot was much more confused. Abraham knew that investing in cities that had no future was a waste of time and energy. He wanted to bear witness to the great hope he had in Christ: the hope of a new creation, a heavenly home, a city with permanent, everlasting foundations made by the living God Himself.

A foundational choice

> The LORD had said to Abram, 'Go from your country,
> your people and your father's household to the land I will
> show you. I will make you into a great nation, and I will
> bless you; I will make your name great, and you will be
> a blessing. I will bless those who bless you, and whoever
> curses you I will curse; and all peoples on earth will be
> blessed through you.' So Abram went, as the LORD had told
> him; and Lot went with him. Abram was seventy-five years
> old when he set out from Harran. He took his wife Sarai,
> his nephew Lot, all the possessions they had accumulated
> and the people they had acquired in Harran, and they set
> out for the land of Canaan, and they arrived there. Abram
> travelled through the land as far as the site of the great tree
> of Moreh at Shechem. At that time the Canaanites were in
> the land. The LORD appeared to Abram and said, 'To your
> seed I will give this land.' So he built an altar there to the
> LORD, who had appeared to him. From there he went on
> toward the hills east of Bethel and pitched his tent, with
> Bethel on the west and Ai on the east. There he built an
> altar to the LORD and called on the name of the LORD.
> (Gen. 12:1-8)

Abram was told to leave everything that he had known and go
to an unidentified destination. Right away he had to make a
choice. The LORD had appeared before his very eyes and called
him into a divine, but unseen future. On the other hand, he
could settle for the seen, tangible, earthly situation he had right
then. Given all the possessions and people with him we can
well imagine he had a sizable stake in Ur of the Chaldees.

Joshua tells us that he was part of a pagan family with all the hopes and dreams, practices and rituals of such religion:

> This is what the LORD, the God of Israel, says: 'Long ago your ancestors, including Terah the father of Abraham and Nahor, lived beyond the Euphrates River and worshipped other gods.' (Josh. 24:2)

The LORD who appeared to him promised Abram a very different future. Through him the whole earth would be blessed. He was told that the Messiah Himself, the Promised Seed, would be his descendant and the destiny of everybody in the world would be determined by Him.

Like Moses, Abraham, Isaac and Jacob saw Him who is invisible (Heb. 11:27).

They saw **everything** in a different way because they saw Him.

What did he set his mind and heart on?

What did Abram long for? What did he set his heart and mind on? Abram longed to see the day of Jesus Christ. He did see it and he was glad (John 8:56). In Genesis 15, the Word of the LORD showed Abram the night sky and promised that He Himself would be Abram's very great reward.

Abram rejected his earthly, passing home in favour of a heavenly, new creation home that Christ the LORD had promised him. He did find a new earthly home in the land of Palestine. He found a place to pitch his tent and moved about, like his sons and grandsons, in the place the LORD had guided him towards. But the very fact that Abraham,

Isaac and Jacob continued to live in their tents rather than building houses and cities proved they were determined not to focus on this passing age.

When faced with the possibility of urban living in Palestine (Gen. 13:18), 'Abram went to live near the great trees of Mamre at Hebron, where he pitched his tents. There he built an altar to the LORD.'

If all they wanted was a stable, solid earthly home they could easily have travelled back to Ur of the Chaldees and lived a prosperous life in the up-and-coming Babylonian superpower.

They knew the LORD had brought them to that promised land, not to find a final home but so they could know Him and be part of His great everlasting future.

Living in tents in that way must have been a difficult choice when they had the resources to put down substantial roots for the remaining years of their mortal life. Yet, they were looking for a true, everlasting home: a city with foundations, built by God Himself.

Looking for a literal resurrection

They were utterly captivated by their resurrection hope. They knew the physical bodies they had in this passing age would be literally resurrected to everlasting life right here in a renewed earth.

It is vital to see how serious they were about burying their bodies. They wanted to make sure they were buried in the very land that the Seed Himself would be born in. They wanted to bear witness to the sure and certain hope that they had in Christ's resurrection.

The whole of Genesis 23 is taken up with finding a place to bury Sarah in the promised land. After a hugely entertaining negotiation process:

> Abraham buried his wife Sarah in the cave in the field of Machpelah near Mamre (which is at Hebron) in the land of Canaan. So the field and the cave in it were deeded to Abraham by the Hittites as a burial site. (Gen. 23:19-20)

Notice that Abraham buried Sarah near to Mamre where he had camped for so long and where they had enjoyed that meal with the LORD back in Genesis 18. He wanted Sarah's body to be buried in the sure and certain hope of the resurrection to eternal life.

Is death the end of the story?

The pagan and atheistic mindset says that once our bodies have died, that is the end of the story. They genuinely believe there is no possible future for this flesh and bone once death has taken hold. But Abraham, Isaac, Jacob and Joseph go to great lengths to proclaim that these bodies are to be taken seriously – even after death.

Of course bodies turn back to dust, whether slowly in the ground or rapidly in fire, but the way the Christian regards those remains is quite different. For us, those bodies will all be called back, re-formed by the God of resurrection. In so many ways we want to mark the places where we bury our loved ones – with gravestones, with plaques on the wall, with memorials, with trees planted at the spot. We want the world to know, and to remind ourselves, that these bodies are not finished – they will be required again.

In Genesis 25 Isaac and Ishmael ensure Abraham is buried in the same way, making the same statement of resurrection hope:

> Abraham lived a hundred and seventy-five years. Then Abraham breathed his last and died at a good old age, an old man and full of years; and he was gathered to his people. His sons Isaac and Ishmael buried him in the cave of Machpelah near Mamre, in the field of Ephron son of Zohar the Hittite, the field Abraham had bought from the Hittites. There Abraham was buried with his wife Sarah. (Gen. 25:7-10)

If the Bible was concerned only with 'the immortality of the soul' – with our living on in some ghostly form in heaven – all this concern with burying bodies would seem very strange. Why be interested at all in a dead, decaying lump of flesh, unless the body has a definite future?

It is the extraordinary good news of Jesus that stands over the bodies of the saints insisting that one day the body will be reconstituted and live on forever and ever. When we trust Jesus the way we look at our bodies is changed. As we look at our hands and feet, as we stare into the mirror and see that body through the years, we know that it will one day be transformed to glorious resurrection perfection and it will never again see decay.

The great burials of Genesis

In Genesis 35:8 Deborah, Rebekah's nurse, dies and she too is buried, this time at the oak tree near to Bethel. In Genesis 35:16-20 Rachel dies giving birth to Benjamin and is buried at Bethlehem. Each of these great saints was buried at a place of great significance, as if they wanted to be raised on the last day right where all the action had taken place!

When Abel was murdered by Cain we are told that his blood cried out from the ground (Gen. 4:10).

These saints also wanted their bodies to testify to the resurrection even after they had left them behind.

In Hebrews 11, in the gallery of the faithful saints, Jacob does not get much mention but one of the two things singled out for him is the way that he made his burial arrangements:

> Jacob lived in Egypt seventeen years, and the years of his life were a hundred and forty-seven. When the time drew near for Israel to die, he called for his son Joseph and said to him, 'If I have found favour in your eyes, put your hand under my thigh and promise that you will show me kindness and faithfulness. Do not bury me in Egypt, but when I rest with my fathers, carry me out of Egypt and bury me where they are buried.' 'I will do as you say,' he said. 'Swear to me,' he said. Then Joseph swore to him, and Israel worshipped as he leaned on the top of his staff. (Gen. 47:28-31)

Jacob wanted to make sure that his body was in the promised land, buried in the place where the Promised Saviour would be born and minister, in the place he wanted to wake on resurrection morning.

His burial is a major event at the end of Genesis, running from Genesis 49:29 right through to 50:14. The whole senior government of Egypt is involved as his mummified body is taken, with great solemnity, to the burial plot near Mamre which Abraham spent the whole of Genesis chapter 23 buying. We can well imagine the words that Joseph spoke as they finally buried Jacob:

> Forasmuch as it hath pleased Almighty God of His great mercy to take unto Himself the soul of our dear brother here departed, we therefore commit His body to the ground; earth to earth, ashes to ashes, dust to dust; in sure and certain hope of the Resurrection to eternal life, through our Lord Jesus Christ; who shall change our vile body, that it may be like unto His glorious body, according to the mighty working, whereby He is able to subdue all things to Himself. [1]

The final verse of Genesis is a verse full of gospel hope and faith, a proclamation of resurrection hope. It is a testimony that this story has much more to come:

> So Joseph died at the age of a hundred and ten. And after they embalmed him, he was placed in a coffin in Egypt. (Gen. 50:26)

Moses' mysterious burial

The burial of Moses himself is perhaps the most mysterious and incredible of all. If we think that all these burial concerns were just the cultural obsessions of some ancient people and do not have quite so much theological depth to them, then the burial of Moses turns us upside down:

> Moses climbed Mount Nebo from the plains of Moab to the top of Pisgah, across from Jericho. There the LORD showed

---

1. From the burial service in the Book of Common Prayer of the Church of England.

him the whole land – from Gilead to Dan, all of Naphtali, the territory of Ephraim and Manasseh, all the land of Judah as far as the western sea, the Negev and the whole region from the Valley of Jericho, the City of Palms, as far as Zoar. Then the LORD said to him, 'This is the land I promised on oath to Abraham, Isaac and Jacob when I said, "I will give it to your descendants." I have let you see it with your eyes, but you will not cross over into it.' And **Moses the servant of the LORD died there in Moab, as the LORD had said. He buried him in Moab, in the valley opposite Beth Peor, but to this day no one knows where his grave is**. Moses was a hundred and twenty years old when he died, yet his eyes were not weak nor his strength gone. The Israelites grieved for Moses in the plains of Moab thirty days, until the time of weeping and mourning was over. (Deut. 34:1-8)

The LORD was so concerned about the burial arrangements of His people that He buried Moses Himself! It is hard to imagine a greater affirmation of the importance of burying a body.

Other resurrection signposts

In the long litany of death in Genesis 5, Enoch was set up as a sign that death does not have to be the final word over the human body. In Genesis 5:3 we are told that Adam had a son in his own image and likeness. Tragically Adam's own sin and death were also in that son. Each section ends in the same relentless way: 'and then he died.' Yet when we come to verse 21 the reign of death is interrupted and challenged:

When Enoch had lived sixty-five years, he became the father of Methuselah. And after he became the father of Methuselah, Enoch walked with God 300 years and had other sons and daughters. Altogether, Enoch lived 365 years. Enoch walked with God; then he was no more, because God took him away. (Gen. 5:21-24)

We know that Enoch himself was straining forward to that last day when Jesus returns in great glory to judge the world and apply His resurrection to the whole world:

Enoch, the seventh from Adam, prophesied about them: 'See, the Lord is coming with thousands upon thousands of his holy ones to judge everyone, and to convict all of them of all the ungodly acts they have committed in their ungodliness, and of all the defiant words ungodly sinners have spoken against him.' (Jude 14-15)

Enoch was taken away to that highest heaven, preserved as a statement that death would be defeated by the Coming Lord. It is amazing to think that there are at least two people in the highest heaven who were born as mortal, sinful human beings like us, whose bodies knew the suffering and decay that we experience – but who did not experience death. We will consider Elijah later!

In Deuteronomy 29:5 we are told that during the 40 years of wandering through the desert the clothes and shoes of the entire church community were immune from decay. It was a miraculous testimony to the life we will live in our resurrection future: a new creation freed from the bondage to decay, a future where things really do last forever.

Leviticus ends with this glorious vision of a world filled with the holiness and glory of God. All the way through the book we see how there was just a tiny space in the tabernacle that was defined as holy, the place where the LORD's presence was found. But in Leviticus 27 we are shown a vision of the church family dedicating fields, houses, animals and people to the LORD. It is as if the holiness of the tabernacle, the glorious presence of the LORD Himself, spills out and spreads across the world. (Remember that in Leviticus in the presence of the LORD there is no death or disease, no decay or sin).

The book ends with this yearning for that day of resurrection when the presence of the LORD will flood the whole world and 'cure' or cleanse the world of death, disease, decay and sin – forever.

The day of atonement

However, perhaps the most intense expression of this resurrection hope, the hope of a new heavens and a new earth, comes in Leviticus 16 – with the day of atonement:

> Aaron shall bring the bull for his own sin offering to make atonement for himself and his household, and he is to slaughter the bull for his own sin offering. He is to take a censer full of burning coals from the altar before the LORD and two handfuls of finely ground fragrant incense and take them behind the curtain. He is to put the incense on the fire before the LORD, and the smoke of the incense will conceal the atonement cover above the Testimony, so that he will not die. He is to take some of the bull's blood and

with his finger sprinkle it on the front of the atonement cover; then he shall sprinkle some of it with his finger seven times before the atonement cover. He shall then slaughter the goat for the sin offering for the people and take its blood behind the curtain and do with it as he did with the bull's blood: He shall sprinkle it on the atonement cover and in front of it. In this way he will make atonement for the Most Holy Place because of the uncleanness and rebellion of the Israelites, whatever their sins have been. He is to do the same for the Tent of Meeting, which is among them in the midst of their uncleanness. No-one is to be in the Tent of Meeting from the time Aaron goes in to make atonement in the Most Holy Place until he comes out, having made atonement for himself, his household and the whole community of Israel. (Lev. 16:11-17)

A radical overhaul!

Jesus Christ is nothing less than the logic and life of the universe and as such will not have any half-baked or temporary solutions to its problems.

He did not come to merely postpone death or provide some temporary comfort in the difficulties of this passing age. His great mission is to bring about such a profound revolution that there will be no death at all; a universe in which nobody needs comforting because there simply isn't any death, pain, sorrow or crying.

The radical revolution of Jesus begins right now and changes our living right here and now but it is geared towards the complete overthrow of this present order: a revolution that changes the character of existence itself across the whole universe.

In one sense we could say that Jesus wants to tear up the laws of nature and write new ones.

A property dealer in London was selling an old warehouse. The property had been badly vandalised and had clearly been used as a squat. There was graffiti on the walls; the windows were broken; paint on the walls was discoloured and peeling; pools of dubious and dark liquids gathered suspiciously on the ground floor.

The property dealer, showing a prospective buyer around, was clearly very embarrassed. Trying to stand in a such a way that he was blocking the buyer's view of the very worst of the mess, he said, 'Look, I'm going to get someone in to fix the windows and give the place a lick of paint… and maybe someone could come and…'

The buyer interrupted him. 'Don't bother with any of that! I'm going to gut the whole lot and make it new.'

Jesus, the eternal Son of the Father, the omnipotent Logos, has very grand plans for His inheritance. He is not in the business of patching up. He deals with resurrection and new creation rather than superficial makeovers!

When Jesus lived among us, He told us in all His words and actions that He was capable and determined to abolish this present darkness and bring about a renewed creation from which all our enemies are evicted.

He showed us that death, disease, demons and decay were all under His complete control. He could abolish them with a word. The chaos and darkness He originally dealt with at creation was proof. He showed that He alone was capable of throwing out the chaos, darkness and death and shutting them out for ever and ever.

His mission is to not merely **improve** but to fundamentally change the whole of reality, from top to bottom.

But how?

Even assuming that God the Son has all the power and competence to accomplish such a mission impossible, just how is this to be done?

With that property developer we know he would need to gain legal ownership of the land and planning permission from the local authority. He would need to employ a team to obliterate the warehouse and get in architects and builders to construct something new. We understand the process. We can see what needs to be done to bring about a mini-revolution for an old warehouse.

But, what about the universe as a whole? **How** can the owner of the universe bring about such a purification and redevelopment of the heavens and the earth?

What needs to be done? What is the method of cosmic re-birth?

Everything planned in detail – in advance

Let's spend some time thinking through the most thorough explanation of all that the Son of God was going to do – Leviticus 16.

Everything that Jesus did after He became flesh was planned for and described in detail in advance in the Law. His work as the anointed King, Prophet and Priest was laid down and explained carefully so that it would be clearly understood both by Himself and the rest of us.

The two rooms of the tabernacle

> When Christ came as high priest of the good things that are already here, he went through the greater and more perfect tabernacle that is not man-made, that is to say, not a part of this creation. He did not enter by means of the blood of goats and calves; but he entered the Most Holy Place once for all by his own blood, having obtained eternal redemption. (Heb. 9:11-12)

If we were to read these words without any knowledge of the Hebrew Scriptures we might well feel a little ignorant. However, having come fresh from Leviticus 16 our minds are full of the background to what Hebrews 9 is talking about.

The tabernacle was the tent-structure that was the centre, geographically and socially and spiritually, of the ancient church in the Old Testament. The tabernacle was a simple structure that had two rooms: the larger Holy Place and the smaller Most Holy Place.

The smaller Most Holy Place contained the Ark of the Covenant (made famous for most people by Indiana Jones). The LORD sat enthroned on this Ark of the Covenant. That inner room was utterly inaccessible, utterly forbidden for any normal person. In fact, it was completely out of bounds for even the priests who constantly worked at the tabernacle.

Only the High Priest can enter

Only the High Priest was allowed into this inner room and then only once a year on the special day described in Leviticus 16 – the day of Atonement, *Yom Kippur*.

The inner room, the Holiest of Holies, was a small cube-shaped room with the Ark of the Covenant in it. It represented heaven, the throne room of the universe.

This is of deep importance if we are to understand the ascension of Jesus. The LORD gave this 3-D representation of the structure of the universe precisely so that we would be able to understand all that God the Son was going to do.

So, on just that one special day of the year the High Priest would symbolically go into heaven in order to make atonement:

> He (the High Priest) shall then slaughter the goat for the sin offering for the people and take its blood behind the curtain and do with it as he did with the bull's blood: He shall sprinkle it on the atonement cover and in front of it. In this way he will make atonement for the Most Holy Place because of the uncleanness and rebellion of the Israelites, whatever their sins have been. He is to do the same for the Tent of Meeting, which is among them in the midst of their uncleanness. No one is to be in the Tent of Meeting from the time Aaron goes in to make atonement in the Most Holy Place until he comes out, having made atonement for himself, his household and the whole community of Israel. (Lev. 16:15-17)

Waiting…

The high priest would symbolically go into heaven on that special day… perform his work of atonement for the tabernacle itself… and then everybody waited for him to come out again.

Did you notice that? No one is to be in the Tent of Meeting from the time Aaron goes in to make atonement in the Most Holy Place until he comes out, having made atonement for himself, his household and the whole community of Israel (Lev. 16:17).

None of the priests were allowed into even the outer room while the High Priest was in the inner room. When the High Priest was doing his priestly work in the Most Holy Place **no other priestly work was permitted**. The whole assembly of Israel simply had to wait, offering no sacrifices of their own, attempting no priestly work of their own.

They waited for him to emerge again.

Jesus takes His own blood into heaven for us

When Christ came as high priest of the good things that are already here, he went through the greater and more perfect tabernacle that is not man-made, that is to say, not a part of this creation. He did not enter by means of the blood of goats and calves; but he entered the Most Holy Place once for all by his own blood, having obtained eternal redemption. (Heb. 9:11-12)

Jesus the divine High Priest took His own blood into heaven. He has gone in, through the curtain to the 'inner room' of the creation, into heaven. That is what happened at the ascension of Jesus.

In the symbolic day of atonement the High Priest would re-emerge from the inner room after a fairly short time. But we are still waiting for the real, divine High Priest to emerge from the real inner room, heaven itself.

Our great High Priest, the one who represents us all, the one who embodies the whole creation, has gone into the Most Holy Place, the throne room of heaven and we are waiting for Him to come back out.

While we are waiting for Him, we need to keep Leviticus 16:17 in mind. There is no more priestly work to be done: no priestly work allowed. We are not permitted to offer any sacrifices of our own. The sacrifice of the High Priest is all-encompassing and sufficient.

If we were to try to make some other sacrifice or try to approach heaven in some other way it would show that we were not trusting and waiting for *the* Great High Priest to come back.

How will He come out?

It is not until verse 28 of Hebrews 9 that we hear about the way He will come out of heaven.

> Christ was sacrificed once to take away the sins of many people; and he will appear a second time, not to bear sin, but to bring salvation to those who are waiting for him. (Heb. 9:28)

His blood has made atonement for the heaven and the earth. When He re-emerges He will cleanse and renew the whole creation.

C. S. Lewis speaks of the ascension of Jesus in this way:

> The Bible says – Jesus says – that He **goes** 'to prepare a place for us.' This presumably means that He is about to create that whole new Nature which will provide the environment or conditions for His glorified humanity and, in Him, for ours...

It is not the picture of an *escape* from any and every kind of Nature into some unconditioned and utterly transcendent life. It is the picture of a new human nature, and a new Nature in general, being brought into existence. We must, indeed, believe the risen body to be… different from the mortal body: but the existence, in the new state, of anything that could in any sense be described as 'body' at all, involves in the long run a whole new universe. **That is the picture – not of unmaking but of remaking**. The old field of space, time, matter and the senses is to be weeded, dug and sown for a new crop. **We** may be tired of that old field: **God is not**.[2]

In one very real sense, our whole life now is a life of waiting, of yearning, of daily praying 'Your Kingdom come'. Yes, there is much for us to do as we hold out the word of life to those who don't know what is happening, to those who still rebel against Him. We show the way, the truth and the life of Jesus as we serve others, as He would do. We care for the needy and love one another. Yet, the heart of what is happening to the universe right now is **waiting**.

As the disciples watched Him wondrously entering into the heavenly inner room, the time of special waiting had begun, the time of the last days. There is nothing more to be done now except for the High Priest to re-emerge and return to the earth to renew the heavens and the earth.

Our man in heaven

In an election the great hope is to send a man to the centre of power, from where he can sort everything out. I've been

2. C. S. Lewis, 'Miracles', Harper One, London, 2015, p. 149.

looking at election slogans from across the world, and the common aspiration in so many is the idea that if we can only get 'our man' into the seat of power then everything can be changed.

'Making the world a better place'.

'A chicken in every pot'.

Way back in ancient Rome, Cato the elder rallied support by endlessly shouting the simple, brutal slogan: 'Carthage must be destroyed'. (I love Cato for that!)

With a very different tone – 'a kinder, gentler nation'. Perhaps the most blunt is simply this – 'If you want a better world, send me to government'.

We do have a man that represents us. He has gone to the government of the universe with a clear and guaranteed manifesto. 'Our man' has gone into the control room, the source of the life and power of the universe. The God-Man who has joined Himself to this created universe has gone to the source of the universe to put the whole thing right.

If the mission of God the Son is to get Himself a bride and prepare His creation as the family home for all eternity then He must get to the source, the foundation, the centre in order to make it all what He wants it to be: a place where death, pain, sorrow and sin have been abolished from every last corner.

So, we await the moment when He will re-emerge from behind the curtain, bringing with Him the whole life and power and light and glory of that heavenly realm. He will come and make the kingdoms of this world the kingdom of God and He will burn away all the powers of evil.

Our great High Priest will re-emerge from that inner room and extend to the whole universe the life that we have seen so wonderfully and gloriously lived among us 2,000 years ago – a life that has no place for death, disease, sin, pain or confusion.

'The term is over: the holidays have begun. The dream is ended: this is the morning.'

And as He spoke, He no longer looked to them like a lion; but the things that began to happen after that were so great and beautiful that I cannot write them. And for us this is the end of all the stories, and we can most truly say that they all lived happily ever after. But for them it was only the beginning of the real story. All their life in this world and all their adventures in Narnia had only been the cover and the title page: now at least they were beginning Chapter One of the Great Story which no one on earth has read: which goes on for ever: in which every chapter is better than the one before.[3]

---

3. C. S. Lewis – *The Last Battle*.

CHAPTER 5

THROUGH DEATH INTO LIFE EVERLASTING

THE first five books of the Bible set the theological foundations. When we come to study heaven and hell in the former prophets, we find them building on all that has gone before.

The book of Joshua provides the general structure for this collection of books. It shows vividly how the whole world is under the judgement of death and destruction, yet there is a new creation future for those who trust in the Divine Joshua, the Commander of the Hosts of Heaven.

After Joshua the histories take us through the ways in which the saints and their leaders either grasp on to heaven here on earth, looking forward to the new creation as they walk in the Spirit with Christ set before them, or how they wander into the darkness and feel the grip of hell as they wait for final judgement.

An overview of the former prophets
– paradise lost and found

The land has a big role to play throughout the Scriptures. It is one of the major gospel signs right from Abraham through to the birth of Jesus Himself. Remember the whole creation is supposed to be one single unified whole with the Garden of God at the centre, providing living water from the throne of God on His glorious mountain.

Adam and Eve fell. They were driven away from paradise, driven to the **east** – into exile. The LORD told Abraham to travel to the **west**, symbolically travelling back to paradise.

Of course, we can't get into heaven simply by travelling far enough west! But symbolically, that journey is the great story of the Bible itself. Just as the sun rises in the east and travels to the west, so the journey of the church from Babylon in the east to the promised land of Canaan in the west is the story of how Jesus takes His people from the exile of death and sin back to paradise itself, the city of God, Zion, and on into the new creation future when heaven and earth will once again be a single, unified whole.

In these books we see the judgement and possession of Canaan, the church in the land but far from the LORD, and then the church driven back to Babylon in exile. With Abraham the Babylonian the church travels out of Babylon, but then ends up back in Babylon in exile.

All the time we are learning deep gospel lessons about Jesus Christ and His redemption of the creation – His work of not only fixing what Adam did wrong but also taking the creation on to its full and final form of immortality where even the Father Himself will live forever and ever.

The land is only a symbol of that final form of the creation. Most of the time it is a very mixed and messy symbol, because of all the sin, compromise and rebellion of the ancient church. And yet if we are going to understand what is happening through the former prophets, we need to keep this deep perspective in mind. We are being taught about the paradise we have lost but also about the new creation future that Christ will bring us to at His coming in glory.

Provoking strong reactions

The book of Joshua provokes strong reactions. When people complain about 'genocide' in the Bible they are really complaining about Joshua. In this book Joshua comes with all the holy ones with him. He is ordered to bring the total and comprehensive judgement of the living God on whole people groups living in the land of Canaan.

He is ordered to kill everybody, including the men, women and children.

Why does the LORD God order such things? Isn't the world filled with enough of that kind of evil without deliberately adding to it? Isn't the divine Joshua, Jesus of Nazareth, defined by turning the other cheek and loving His enemies?

A preview of that great and terrible final day

If there is any book of the Bible that really takes us into the theology and experience of the final day of judgement then it is this book. It confronts us with the great new creation hope but also with the very real destruction of the wicked on that day that Jesus comes in great glory with all His holy ones with Him.

On that great and terrible day of the LORD, Jesus will destroy every man, woman and child in the world who has not found refuge in Him.

A day of reckoning

This is good news! There is a day of reckoning, a day when everything will be put right. Old western films often begin with some terrible wrong being committed and the hero, muttering, 'There will be a reckoning for this.'

When we hear of the evil in the world and those who really need help being forgotten and crushed, even we cry out – 'something must be done! There must be a reckoning!' When it comes even closer to home, the anger, the pain is too much to bear. How can we get relief? We can see why some people try to take matters into their own hands, one way or another, while others simply fall apart.

The fact we think and feel like this is a pale shadow of how the living God thinks and feels. The eternal Father, Son and Spirit have seen the whole history of humanity and seen all this evil.

Even now it is provoking the Living and Holy God.

If we have ever been present in the aftermath of real evil and heard the cries of anguish, the anger, the despair, the pain, then we have been given a small glimpse into the heart of the living God. How could we ever ask why He is angry about the world?

There are times in the Bible when God speaks as if He has had enough and He simply wants to destroy the world, including those who are supposed to be His people. In spite of feeling such outrage, this gracious and patient God has set a date for the day of justice. He has borne this anger all too long and now He waits for that final day when everything can be put right.

On that day the world will be set right. Those who embrace His way and truth and life will be welcomed into His new creation and enjoy His kingdom of love, peace and justice forever. Those who refuse Him will no longer be allowed to live in His world and will be thrown into the outer darkness. There will be no escape for anybody. No exceptions will be made. Nobody will be able to buy their way out of justice or bribe their way out of prison.

Far from being some kind of sick manual for human warfare or an apology for 'genocide', the book of Joshua is an account of how at one time, long ago, the LORD God gave a preview of that final day.

A day of justice

The nations who lived in Canaan had been getting progressively worse and worse down the generations. The worship of their gods involved human sacrifice, even throwing babies into the fire.[1] In spite of all this, the LORD waited and waited in the hope that perhaps they would turn away from that way of death towards life. He kept His church in slavery in Egypt for hundreds of years in order that these Canaanite people would have more opportunity to change – and yet things got worse and worse.[2]

One person commented that if any nation in the world today was publically and routinely throwing children into

---

1. Leviticus 20:1-5; Deuteronomy 18:10-11.
2. Genesis 15:12-16.

the fire we would expect and even campaign for the United Nations to intervene, with military force if necessary. The book of Joshua is the written record of that kind of action taking place in an age when such a response was unheard of.

The time came when the LORD God imposed a kind of day of justice on the land of Canaan. The day of reckoning had come. The LORD sent His appointed man, Joshua, to enact this judgement. It was not a general guide to warfare for any other generation or any other nation, yet at that time the LORD God authorised Joshua to utterly destroy those specific Canaanite groups.[3] It was a terrible judgement to fall on an entire population, yet it was a very vivid picture of how it will be on that final day.

Listen to these words from the book of Revelation describing how it will be for the whole world when the LORD leads His angelic armies against this dark world:

> The kings of the earth, the princes, the generals, the rich, the mighty, and every slave and every free man hid in caves and among the rocks of the mountains. They called to the mountains and the rocks, 'Fall on us and hide us from the face of him who sits on the throne and from the wrath of the Lamb! For the great day of their wrath has come, and who can stand?' (Rev. 6:15-17)

If we are to really understand why the Living God ordained the events of the book of Joshua to happen and why the Holy Spirit recorded these extraordinary events for us, we need to approach the book in the full context of the whole Bible,

---

3. See Deuteronomy 7:1-6.

understanding this special book in the way it was originally intended.

Only hope – the sign of blood

After the commissioning of Joshua we are told a wonderful gospel story, placed right at the beginning, to make sure that we understand what we must do.

When the spies are sent to check out the land, Rahab repents from her old life and joins herself to Israel. She has heard of the LORD and knows there is no way to resist Him or avoid His coming judgement. To use Jesus' words from Luke 14:32, she asks for terms of peace:

> The LORD your God is God in heaven above and on the earth below. Now then, please swear to me by the LORD that you will show kindness to my family, because I have shown kindness to you. Give me a sure sign that you will spare the lives of my father and mother, my brothers and sisters, and all who belong to them, and that you will save us from death. (Josh. 2:11-13)

We have seen how the plagues of Egypt were a careful explanation of the barren, dark and lifeless nature of hell, cut off from God. They led up to the final judgement of death when the LORD Himself brought death on every house that did not shelter under the blood of the Passover lamb. The LORD passed through Egypt and if the sign of blood was on a house He passed over it. They were safe.

Rahab was told to place the sign of blood on her house. When this earthly Jesus (Joshua son of Nun) came on His earthly day of judgement, her household would be safe. She has to tie a scarlet cord in the window, marking her house with the scarlet sign just as the houses were marked with the scarlet sign of blood in the Passover. On that day her home would be an Israelite home.

That story is so important. God had placed all the people of Jericho under the sentence of death: total destruction. The armies of the LORD were assembling to enact that final judgement. Yet, even then, even when the day of judgement was approaching, there was still a way out.

We need to hear this truth. The day of justice is very near. The night is far spent and the morning is at hand. Even before you finish this chapter the day of justice may be here, the trumpet will sound and the armies of heaven will descend to do to this world on a cosmic level what was done to Jericho so long ago.

If that scarlet sign is on us, if that sign of blood is over us, we will be safe. It's not too late. Even now, we can sue for peace and join the church of God.

Crossing the Jordan

The crossing of the Jordan in Joshua chapter 3 has long had deep significance for the saints of Christ down the generations. The people had been wandering in exile for a generation and now they are standing on the brink of the river. We can see how powerful this moment is.

Right from the time of Abraham, some 400 years previously, the LORD had promised a land, an inheritance for the saints. Abraham, Isaac and Jacob had experienced something of it, though it had been occupied by the pagan Canaanites. They had properly owned just one small burial plot where they could bear witness to their great resurrection hope.

Samples of heaven and hell right now

This physical land of Canaan had been promised to them as a sample of that full resurrection hope.

Heaven and hell, new creation and outer darkness, are not just far off ideas in the distant future. Already, right here and now, we may experience heaven and hell on earth, in our own hearts and minds.

Samples of heaven and hell touch human life all the time. We can experience the presence of the living God, through Jesus in the power of the Spirit, even right now as we live in His world. Church is supposed to be heaven on earth every time we gather together. In His mercy He might give us some experiences of the blessings of this world: food, friendship, a home, land, health and community. When we taste these blessings in fellowship with Him, sharing our possessions with the church family, we are given a sample of that new creation inheritance that lies before us.

On the other hand, when sin controls us, when futile pagan thinking grips us and darkness enslaves us within, when despair, guilt and decay overwhelm us, when we see and experience sin, when evil is allowed to rule, when we are alienated from the life of God then we experience a sample of hell itself.

Standing on the edge of the Jordan the ancient church was standing in the old land of exile, hardship and wandering, yet they could see the land of promise in front of them. They knew that across that river there was a land of plenty, flowing with milk and honey and it had been promised to them!

Resurrection hope in the face of death

The way they cross is remarkable. They cross (Josh. 3:2) 'after three days' which immediately puts on alert that we are dealing with an event of resurrection hope in the face of death. 1 Corinthians 15:4 reminds us that Jesus rose on the third day 'according to the Scriptures', alerting us to the fact that the pattern of resurrection or new life on the third day is embedded deep in the Bible.

The Jordan was in full flood at that time of the year (v. 15). It was the hardest time to cross. God wanted them to trust Him to make it safe to cross. The ark of the covenant, held by the priests, went first – the ark where the angel of the LORD sat enthroned among them during all their wilderness wandering. He would make a safe path for them. As soon as the ark got to the flooded Jordan the water stopped and they were able to cross.

Perhaps the most striking thing about this incident comes in verses 16 and 17:

> …the water from upstream stopped flowing. It piled up in a heap a great distance away, at a town called Adam in the vicinity of Zarethan, while the water flowing down to the Sea of the Arabah (the Salt Sea) was completely cut off. So the people crossed over opposite Jericho. The priests who carried the ark of the covenant of the LORD stood firm on dry ground in the middle of the Jordan, while all Israel passed by until the whole nation had completed the crossing on dry ground.

The river flowed from **Adam** down to the Salt Sea. Salt is a sign of judgement in the Bible (remember Lot's wife turned into a pillar of salt on Sodom and Gomorrah's day of judgement). Adam brought death on us, cutting us off from the dwelling of God, and that river of death has flowed down continuously ever since to the Salt Sea of judgement. Yet, when the ark with its atonement cover stands in the river, the water stops.

In this powerful symbol the river that cut them off from the promised land, the river that prevented them going west from their exile, was stopped at Adam by the LORD Himself.

A powerful image of the death of the Christian

Joshua chapter 3 has been a powerful image for the death of Christians down the ages. We are still living in the wilderness wanderings of this passing age, yet just ahead of us, just across that river, is our heavenly home.

William Williams, the great hymn writer and theologian, expressed it more famously than anyone else:

> When I tread the verge of Jordan,
> bid my anxious fears subside;
> death of death and hell's destruction,
> land me safe on Canaan's side.
> Songs of praises, songs of praises,
> I will ever give to Thee;
> I will ever give to Thee.

Isaiah 43:2-3 echoes that same thought, 'When you pass through the waters, I will be with you… For I am the LORD your God, the Holy One of Israel, your Saviour'.

John Bunyan ends his wonderful Pilgrim's Progress with this crossing. As the saints cross the river into the celestial city there are all kinds of reactions, but the final one of Mr Standfast is the best one:

> When Mr Standfast had thus set things in order, and the time being come for him to haste him away, he also went down to the river... And he said, This river has been a terror to many; yea, the thoughts of it also have often frightened me; but now methinks I stand easy; my foot is fixed upon that on which the feet of the priests that bare the ark of the covenant stood while Israel went over Jordan. (Josh. 3:17). The waters indeed are to the palate bitter, and to the stomach cold; yet the thoughts of what I am going to, and of the convoy that waits for me on the other side, do lie as a glowing coal at my heart. I see myself now at the end of my journey; my toilsome days are ended. I am going to see that head which was crowned with thorns, and that face which was spit upon for me. I have formerly lived by hearsay and faith; but now I go where I shall live by sight, and shall be with Him in whose company I delight myself. I have loved to hear my Lord spoken of; and wherever I have seen the print of His shoe in the earth, there I have coveted to set my foot too. His name has been to me... sweeter than all perfumes. His voice to me has been most sweet, and His countenance I have more desired than they that have most desired the light of the sun. His words I did use to gather for my food, and for antidotes against my faintings. He hath held me, and hath kept me from mine iniquities; yea, my steps hath He strengthened in His way.

Now, while he was thus in discourse, his countenance changed; his strong man bowed under him: and after he had said, Take me, for I come unto Thee, he ceased to be seen of them.

But glorious it was to see how the open region was filled with horses and chariots, with trumpeters and pipers, with singers and players upon stringed instruments, to welcome the pilgrims as they went up, and followed one another in at the beautiful gate of the city.[4]

The final words of the saints as they cross that river are incredible testimonies to the truth that Joshua 3 proclaims.

Martin Luther [1483-1546], 'Into your hands I commit my spirit; God of truth, you have redeemed me.'

Thomas Cartwright [1535-1603], English Puritan, 'I have found unutterable comfort and happiness, and God has given me a glimpse of heaven.'

Thomas Holland [1539-1612], the English Bible translator, 'Come, O come, Lord you bright Morning Star! Come, Lord! I desire to be dissolved and to be with Jesus, Jesus, you.'

Donald Cargill [1619-1681], Scottish covenanter, 'This is the most joyful day that ever I saw in my pilgrimage on earth. My joy is now begun, which I see shall never be interrupted.'

John Flavel [1627-1691], English Presbyterian preacher, 'I know that it will be well with me.'

Ralph Erskine [1685-1752], Scottish churchman, 'Victory, victory, victory.'

---

4. Bunyan, J. (1995). *The pilgrim's progress : From this world to that which is to come*. Oak Harbor.

Samuel Finley [1715-1766], Scottish preacher, 'I see the eternal love and goodness of God. I see the love of Jesus. Oh, to be dissolved, and to be with Him! I long to be clothed with the complete righteousness of Christ.'

To Dr Waugh one said, 'You are now in the deep Jordan; have you any doubt that Christ will be with you?' He replied, 'Certainly not! Who else? Who else?'

D. H. Gillette: 'O that I had strength to shout! I feel so happy. O, the precious Savior; what is the world to me? All its vanity? Give me Jesus. Do not weep for me, I am going home.'

Alexander Proudfit: 'When will this lingering conflict end? Oh, for a speedy and easy transition! Oh for deliverance from this corruptible body – this body of sin and death! Come, blessed Jesus, dear Savior, come! come! I long to depart.'

Augustus Toplady [1740-1778], hymn writer, 'I believe God never gave such manifestations of his love to any creature, and allowed him to live.'

John Wesley [1703-1791], English preacher, 'The best of all is, God is with us.'

Mrs Hannah More [1745-1833], the great evangelical worker, 'Jesus is all in all. God of grace, God of light, God of love: whom have I in heaven but you? It is a glorious thing to die.' Her last word was, 'Joy.'[5]

A wonderful, glorious book!

Far from being a book filled with misery and destruction, the heart of the book of Joshua is a wonderful, glorious

---

5. These are collected from 'Wanderings of a Pilgrim' by David Harsha, 1856.

book of celebration and joy. This book lays before us the future inheritance of the saints. It is designed to fill us with great confidence about death, judgement and our promised inheritance. Evil will finally be defeated and thrown out. Death need hold no fears for us. Our LORD God will take us to our true home forever, while we wait with Him and on into that final new creation future.

Face down before the true Judge of the world

In the book of Joshua the ancient church was required to bring about the comprehensive judgement on the Canaanite people.

But in Joshua 5 the LORD Jesus personally takes responsibility for the judgements. When Joshua meets the heavenly Joshua, he is left in no doubt as to who the General of this campaign is, the real commander of the LORD's army. He has to take off his shoes and wait for orders as he lies face down before the true judge of the whole world:

> When Joshua was near Jericho, he looked up and saw a man standing in front of him with a drawn sword in his hand. Joshua went up to him and asked, 'Are you for us or for our enemies?'

> 'Neither,' he replied, 'but as Commander of the army of the LORD I have now come.' Then Joshua fell face down to the ground in reverence, and asked him, 'What message does my Lord have for his servant?'

The commander of the LORD's army replied, 'Take off your sandals, for the place where you are standing is holy.' And Joshua did so. (Josh. 5:13-15)

Jericho's destruction – an iconic prophecy

The destruction of Jericho is an iconic prophecy of how the heavenly Joshua will conquer the whole world. Jericho was shut up against the LORD and His people (Josh. 6). It was a sorry sight. These rebels were trying to find a hiding place from the coming judgement and seemed to think that mere stone walls could prevent the LORD from finding them. This is how it will be on that final day as the world calls out for the rocks to hide them from the wrath of the Lamb (Rev. 6:15-17).

Yet, when the Commander of the LORD's army looks down on the city, He tells Joshua, 'See, I have delivered Jericho into your hands, along with its king and its fighting men' (Josh. 6:2). On that day the defences of Jericho were not even worth mentioning. On the last day the world will be defeated by a single breath from Jesus (2 Thess. 2:8).

The details of the conquest take us to the heart of the event. The creation was made in 6 days. So, each day, for 6 days the priests and the people were to simply walk around Jericho.

How strange that would have seemed! The people of Jericho would surely have hurled insults at them. 'Where is this LORD God? Where is this judgement? Things are going on just as they always have. All you can do is walk around the walls in silence!'

Yet, on the seventh day, the day when the LORD entered His rest in the very first week, the land was about to get rest from the pagan pollution that had defiled it.

The priests were to sound seven trumpets and then make a long blast on the ram's horn. Then all the people had to release a great shout. The walls would fall and the victory would be complete.

Surely this is the strangest victory in the whole Bible!

What's going on? How can the sounding of trumpets bring about such a mighty judgement and victory?

The feast of trumpets

In the Pentateuch, we find that on the first day of the seventh month the ancient church had to take a day out for blowing silver trumpets – the feast of trumpets. Why? Because back in Exodus 19 and 20 the sound of the trumpet, or the ram's horn, signaled the coming of God Himself to Mount Sinai. The trumpets declared the power and glory and triumph of Almighty God as heaven came down to earth.

On that final day the trumpet will sound and a great shout will go up as the City of God comes down to earth, as the Father Himself comes to dwell with His people. On that day when the saints take possession of their inheritance there will be no room for the wicked or unbelievers, no matter what secure walls they hide behind.

> The Lord himself will come down from heaven, with a loud command, with the voice of the archangel and with the trumpet call of God, and the dead in Christ will rise first. (1 Thess. 4:16)

The church will inherit the earth

The entire city was burned and the wicked people completely removed from the land as the LORD and His people took possession of their inheritance.

The fact of the matter is that the whole earth belongs to us, the church of the living God. Yes, at the moment we may be at the bottom of the pile and the world seems to belong to the rich and the powerful, the wicked and the worldly. However, everything really belongs to us in Jesus Christ and we are to live our lives with that knowledge and hope.

A day is coming soon when the walls of this old Babylon will be thrown down and the true order of heaven will be imposed on earth. There will be no place for the wicked or greedy or selfish on that day. They will have already enjoyed all the comfort they will ever know. Then, on that day of the heavenly Joshua, the saints will take possession of the earth.

The stories of Jericho and Ai encourage us that the enemies of Christ will be judged and removed when He comes. Nothing will be brushed under the carpet. Nothing will be whitewashed away. There will be no more cover ups. There will be nowhere to hide. No one will escape that day of cleansing and justice. There will be no roots of evil left to spring up later. There will be no refuge for darkness and sin. A day is coming when the whole creation will finally be set free, when the poor and the weak and the oppressed will be welcomed by their LORD into the rich inheritance of the whole creation that He has always planned for them.

Those who see this passing age as their hope and their heaven will always try to ignore or rage against the coming day of justice. They see nothing to look forward to at all, but for those who long for the coming kingdom of God, those who this world hates, the day of justice is a day of great joy.

Now, in this passing age of darkness, those that depend on the LORD may be led like sheep to the slaughter, sacked from their jobs, laughed at and rejected. We follow the commands of Jesus and turn the other cheek, praying only that our enemies may turn around and be saved from the coming day of judgement.

Now, we leave all matters of vengeance to the LORD Himself and do all we can to love our enemies into the kingdom. However, we do this knowing that one day a true order will be given to the universe and justice established over all.

No resurrection

Notice how the city of Ai is judged and destroyed. Hell is not going to be a temporary solution. It is the final home of sin and evil. Hell is the ruin and destruction of all who will not have this Man to rule over them:

> Joshua burned Ai and made it a permanent heap of ruins, a desolate place to this day. He hung the king of Ai on a tree and left him there until evening. At sunset, Joshua ordered them to take his body from the tree and throw it down at the entrance of the city gate. And they raised a large pile of rocks over it, which remains to this day. (Josh. 8:28-29)

The king of Ai died the cursed death of crucifixion, but there was no resurrection for him. Just as his city remained a permanent heap of ruins, so he and all those who followed

123

his ways remain under that cursed death with no way for them to carry on their evil darkness ever again. The stones were rolled in front of his tomb and remain there.

Crushing Satan underfoot

Look at the fate of the Amorite kings in Joshua 10:

> Joshua said, 'Open the mouth of the cave and bring those five kings out to me.' So they brought the five kings out of the cave – the kings of Jerusalem, Hebron, Jarmuth, Lachish and Eglon. When they had brought these kings to Joshua, he summoned all the men of Israel and said to the army commanders who had come with him, 'Come here and put your feet on the necks of these kings.' So they came forward and placed their feet on their necks.
>
> Joshua said to them, 'Do not be afraid; do not be discouraged. Be strong and courageous. This is what the LORD will do to all the enemies you are going to fight.' Then Joshua struck and killed the kings and hung them on five trees, and they were left hanging on the trees until evening.
>
> At sunset Joshua gave the order and they took them down from the trees and threw them into the cave where they had been hiding. At the mouth of the cave they placed large rocks, which are there to this day.
>
> That day Joshua took Makkedah. He put the city and its king to the sword and totally destroyed everyone in it. He left no survivors. And he did to the king of Makkedah as he had done to the king of Jericho. (Josh. 10:22-28)

Notice how the men of Israel put their feet on the necks of these evil kings. These men had crushed people under their own feet for too long. How often had innocent blood cried out to the judge of all the earth? Now, the earthly Joshua brought some justice to the land and they were under the feet of the LORD and His people.

This of course reminds us of the promise made at the very beginning of the Bible when the LORD Jesus pronounced His curse on Satan himself – Genesis 3:14-15. Yet, it is not just Christ who crushes Satan under His feet. His whole church are given the same victory.

> The God of peace will soon crush Satan under your feet. (Rom. 16:20)

The book of Joshua can seem uncomfortable reading for those of us used to a comfortable life free from tyrannical rulers and evil thugs. I have even heard people complain that these Canaanite pagans deserved another chance, that they weren't all that bad. Such a view of history and life can only come from those who have lived in fairly safe communities that still benefit from the Christian legacy of freedom, justice, rule of law, respect and human dignity.

For those who know nothing of this, the book of Joshua is a book filled with such great hope. For those who experience the brutal tyranny of evil men, with their regimes of violence, abuse and greed, the knowledge that the Commander of the LORD's armies is coming to make sure these evil men are crushed underfoot is a great comfort.

What they are and what they have done will be exposed and punished.

The land – shared equally and fairly

Chapters 14-21 of Joshua seem hard to read because they are taken up with the detailed allocation of the land to all the different tribes of Israel. However, if we understand the meaning of the land, we can see why this is given so much space.

In Numbers God had specified that the land had to be shared out equally and fairly, divided by lot to the ancient church. This is exactly what is happening in these long chapters.

Just imagine…

Imagine you are from the tribe of Asher. You've crossed over the Jordan to take possession of the land. For many years you've heard all the promises the LORD has given about your inheritance. You've grown up hearing stories of Abraham, Isaac and Jacob – how the Angel of the LORD appeared with His promise of the Seed and descendants inheriting the land as a sample of the new creation.

The time has come. You've entered the land and marched around Jericho. You've seen the angel of the LORD drive out evil inhabitants. You've seen evil cities destroyed and burned. You've seen wicked kings brought to justice. Your excitement is growing. This is a wonderful land, flowing with milk and honey. Can there really be a part in it for me? Has the LORD really given me a piece?

Finally, Israel gathers at Shiloh (Josh. 18:1). You see Joshua cast lots to divide the land among the tribes, right down to the divisions and families.

Can you imagine what it would be like to finally be told that this plot is now yours? Imagine being shown around that plot of land that had been chosen for you. Imagine being shown the house that is now yours. It must have been amazing!

When the Scriptures describe our new creation hope, it is much more concrete and physical than we realise. In Micah 4, when the mountain of the LORD is joined back to the earth, the saints enter into their new creation inheritance. Then all of us will be given a piece of that eternal 'Canaan' prepared for us by the LORD Himself.

> Everyone will sit under their own vine
> and under their own fig tree,
> and no one will make them afraid,
> for the LORD Almighty has spoken. (Micah 4:4)

We need to think deeply about this. The book of Joshua and then all the books that follow present our new creation hope in very real and concrete terms. Jesus Himself said that He has gone ahead of us to prepare a specific place for each of us who trust in Him (John 14:1-3).

The true glory and joy of heaven and our resurrection future is Jesus Himself, but He will also grant us a real place in His renewed world.

After that resurrection day, after the greatest feast there will ever be, the marriage feast of the Lamb, there will be a time when we will be shown to our own place in the inheritance. We are not anonymous numbers, but genuine, valued members of the body:

> So the LORD gave Israel all the land he had sworn to give
> their forefathers, and they took possession of it and settled

there. The LORD gave them rest on every side, just as he had sworn to their forefathers. Not one of their enemies withstood them; the LORD handed all their enemies over to them. Not one of all the LORD's good promises to the house of Israel failed; every one was fulfilled. (Josh. 21:43-45)

And the other books...

There are many aspects of heaven and hell that we can pick up from the rest of the former prophets with these foundation principles from Joshua firmly in our minds.

Hannah's prayer at the beginning of 1 Samuel is a model of clear hope and confidence concerning the resurrection, the fate of the wicked and Christ's final day of judgement:

> The LORD brings death and makes alive;
> He brings down to the grave and raises up...
> For the foundations of the earth are the LORD's;
> upon them he has set the world.
> He will guard the feet of his saints,
> but **the wicked will be silenced in darkness**.
> It is not by strength that one prevails;
> those who oppose the Lord will be shattered.
> He will thunder against them from heaven;
> the Lord will judge the ends of the earth.
> 'He will give strength to his King
> and exalt the horn of his Christ.'
>
> (1 Sam. 2:6-10)

Before Israel ever had a king, Hannah knew the true King, the Promised Jesus Christ, the One who would judge from heaven, throwing the wicked into the silent darkness yet raising the saints from death.

1 Samuel 28 has a famous incident. Samuel is disturbed from his time in paradise and briefly sent back to the earth to give one more prophecy to Saul. It is an extraordinary event causing endless speculation and controversy among those who enjoy that sort of thing. Saul had banned all mediums and spiritists, yet he wanted to talk to Samuel one last time. This witch from Endor was perhaps more accustomed to demons passing messages to her when she performed her 'magic', but on this occasion she is pushed aside as the real prophet Samuel returns from paradise to speak to Saul. Even though many people speculate about this story, perhaps the most it tells us about heaven is that the saints still live even after their bodies turn to dust.

Yet, if we are studying the former prophets to learn about heaven and hell, there is the glorious moment when the prophet Elijah is taken bodily into heaven by chariots of fire in 2 Kings 2.

Elisha was talking to Elijah about receiving a double dose of the Holy Spirit so that he could carry on his work when (v. 11) 'As they were walking along and talking together, suddenly a chariot of fire and horses of fire appeared and separated the two of them, and Elijah went up to heaven in a whirlwind.'

The hope of the righteous in the face of death is gloriously and wonderfully confirmed. The Bible tells us that the saints are carried to paradise by the angels (Luke 16:22). On this occasion Elisha's eyes were opened to see it all taking place right in front of him! If we are trusting in Jesus, we may also look forward to chariots of fire coming to collect us when we die. What glory!

When David was overwhelmed by the fear of death, he sang a great psalm of praise in 2 Samuel 22.

David sang to the LORD the words of this song when the LORD delivered him from the hand of all his enemies and from the hand of Saul. He said:

> The LORD is my rock, my fortress and my deliverer;
> my God is my rock, in whom I take refuge…
> The waves of death swirled about me;
> the torrents of destruction overwhelmed me.
> The cords of the grave coiled around me;
> the snares of death confronted me.
> In my distress I called to the LORD;
> I called out to my God.
> From his temple he heard my voice;
> my cry came to his ears. (v. 1-7)

David feared that he was falling into that destruction and decay, that emptiness and darkness of death and hell. The Authorised Version translates it as 'the sorrows of hell compassed me about…' But when he called out to the LORD he was given reassurance and confidence in his Saviour.

David could do nothing to save himself from death and hell, yet God was his Saviour and he did not need to be afraid. When he died he knew he would be with the LORD Himself in Zion, the Holy Mountain of God, the heavenly temple. When his baby son died, he had great peace when all around him expected him to be even more grief-stricken.

David explained (2 Sam. 12:23) – 'I will go to him, but he will not return to me.'

Confident of going to Zion, the city of God, where he would again see his dead son, David's psalms are full of this hope of paradise and resurrection future. We will look at those psalms more closely in another chapter.

Are we ready?

Perhaps the best way to conclude is to go back to the book of Joshua. Are we ready to face our own death? Are we ready to cross over the Jordan and enter the heavenly Canaan, to be with the Lord Jesus?

Spurgeon's Morning and Evening Meditation for January 1st.

'They did eat of the fruit of the land of Canaan that year.'
                                                    Joshua 5:12

Israel's weary wanderings were all over, and the promised rest was attained. No more moving tents, fiery serpents, fierce Amalekites, and howling wildernesses: they came to the land which flowed with milk and honey, and they ate the old corn of the land. Perhaps this year, beloved Christian reader, this may be thy case or mine. Joyful is the prospect, and if faith be in active exercise, it will yield unalloyed delight. To be with Jesus in the rest which remaineth for the people of God, is a cheering hope indeed, and to expect this glory so soon is a double bliss. Unbelief shudders at the Jordan which still rolls between us and the goodly land, but let us rest assured that we have already experienced more ills than death at its worst can cause us. Let us banish every fearful thought, and rejoice with exceeding great joy, in the prospect that this year we shall begin to be 'forever with the Lord.'

A part of the host will this year tarry on earth, to do service for their Lord. If this should fall to our lot, there is no reason why the New Year's text should not still be true. 'We who have believed do enter into rest.' The Holy Spirit is the earnest of our inheritance; He gives us 'glory begun below.' In heaven they are secure, and so are we preserved in Christ Jesus; there they triumph over their enemies, and we have victories too. Celestial spirits enjoy communion with their Lord, and this is not denied to us; they rest in His love, and we have perfect peace in Him: they hymn His praise, and it is our privilege to bless Him too. We will this year gather celestial fruits on earthly ground, where faith and hope have made the desert like the garden of the Lord. Man did eat angels' food of old, and why not now? O for grace to feed on Jesus, and so to eat of the fruit of the land of Canaan this year! [6]

---

6. C. H. Spurgeon, 'Morning and Evening', Peabody, MA: Hendrickson Publishers, 2006 – January 1st.

CHAPTER 6

THE DAY OF JUSTICE

IN Billy Joel's song 'Only the good die young' we find a classic doctrine of the world:

> They say there's a heaven for those who wait. Some say it's better, but I say it ain't. I'd rather laugh with the sinners than cry with the saints. Sinners are much more fun…

Heaven and hell should not be taken seriously! The day of judgement will not be a problem! Hell will be more fun than heaven! Mark Twain even wrote that heaven might have the best environment but hell would have the best company!

The latter prophets shatter these delusions and force us to confront the stark truth.

> 'There will be wailing in all the vineyards, for I will pass
> through your midst,' says the LORD.
> Woe to you who long for the day of the LORD!
> Why do you long for the day of the LORD?

That day will be darkness, not light.

It will be as though a man fled from a lion only to meet a
    bear, as though he entered his house and rested his hand
    on the wall only to have a snake bite him.

Will not the day of the LORD be darkness, not light – pitch-
    dark, without a ray of brightness?

(Amos 5:17-21)

The prophets hold the reality of the unseen kingdom of heaven before us, ruled over by the Father, Son and Spirit. They hold up the future hope of the coming day of justice. They even look on beyond to the wonders of the new creation future.

They are so utterly captivated by the unseen reality of the LORD Jesus Christ and His kingdom that all the glory, religion, pleasures and pains of this passing age are shrunk down to the dust compared to the eternal glory and worth of Christ Himself.

The latter prophets can seem overwhelming as they confront not just Israel and Judah but all the nations around them, but it is the certainty of that eternal future that drives and frees them from all fear of mere mortals.

The light switched on!

In the opening chapters of Amos we get the sheer scale and scope of His rejection of the sins of this age and the certainty of the coming day of justice when all will be judged and put right.

Each nation faces destruction by fire because of sin. The sin of all nations reaches its climax in the coming judgement on Judah and Israel (whose guilt is so much worse because of the law they have received from God):

The LORD roars from Zion and thunders from Jerusalem; the pastures of the shepherds dry up, and the top of Carmel withers…

This is what the LORD says: 'For three sins of Edom, even for four, I will not turn back [my wrath]. Because he pursued his brother with a sword, stifling all compassion, because his anger raged continually and his fury flamed unchecked…'

This is what the LORD says: 'For three sins of Ammon, even for four, I will not turn back [my wrath]. Because he ripped open the pregnant women of Gilead in order to extend his borders…'

This is what the LORD says: 'For three sins of Judah, even for four, I will not turn back [my wrath]. Because they have rejected the law of the LORD and have not kept his decrees, because they have been led astray by false gods, the gods their ancestors followed…'

This is what the LORD says: 'For three sins of Israel, even for four, I will not turn back [my wrath]. They sell the righteous for silver, and the needy for a pair of sandals. They trample on the heads of the poor as upon the dust of the ground and deny justice to the oppressed. Father and son use the same girl and so profane my holy name. They lie down beside every altar on garments taken in pledge. In the house of their god they drink wine taken as fines.' (Amos 1:2–2:8)

The coming day of justice is a day when all sin is exposed, when the light is switched on and shines into every secret corner of our dark and sinful lives.

The kingdoms of the earth may go on with their godless and sinful ways of oppression, but above them all is the kingdom of heaven. The Lord Jesus Christ sees all that is happening. These crimes and tragedies might be brushed under the carpet and lost in the mists of human history, but the Judge of all the world has seen it all and will demand an accounting – from everyone.

How can anyone stand?

Yet, how can anyone live if the Holy Judge of heaven is coming in holy, fiery judgement? If His judgement of condemnation and His sentence of death has been passed against us all, how can anyone stand on the day of His appearing?

The strange and wonderful message that comes through these prophets is that the LORD Himself is the way to life, even as He comes to pronounce and execute the sentence of death!

> This is what the LORD says to the house of Israel: 'Seek **me** and live; do not seek Bethel, do not go to Gilgal, do not journey to Beersheba. For Gilgal will surely go into exile, and Bethel will be reduced to nothing. Seek **the LORD** and live, or he will sweep through the house of Joseph like a fire; it will devour, and Bethel will have no one to quench it.' (Amos 5:4-6)

The prophets preach and apply the law of God to the church. They are constantly returning to the stark choice of life and death set before the world in the law. In Christ there is the

136

true life of the Spirit, overflowing in the life of the church, expressed in compassion, truth and joy. The danger is that instead of turning to life through Christ we might continue on in death, deceiving ourselves with mere religion, political security, false prophets and temporary pleasures.

We need to keep Deuteronomy 27 and 28 in mind as we read. The language of the blessings and curses of the law comes up time after time after time. The law was looking at more than just the land of Canaan. It was always looking to the new creation future when Christ will renew the whole creation and pour out those blessings on the new heavens and the new earth.

Superficial religion and ritual is a hindrance not a help.

'Oh, that one of you would shut the temple doors, so that you would not light useless fires on my altar! I am not pleased with you,' says the LORD Almighty, 'and I will accept no offering from your hands. My name will be great among the nations, from the rising to the setting of the sun. In every place incense and pure offerings will be brought to my name, because my name will be great among the nations,' says the LORD Almighty. (Mal. 1:10-11)

Above the chaos and darkness of the human ocean is the eternal rock of Christ the Lord who offers life and stability that is eternal life. Religion and false prophets are part of the broad way of death that keeps us locked into the worthless habits, desires and empty securities that drag us down to hell itself.

The day of the Lord is coming when His true glory will be revealed.

Stunning encounters with Christ

In the depths of exile, far away from the sacraments of the temple and Jerusalem, through the prophets God showed the reality of heaven, the true throne room of the universe, the city of God where the righteous wait. Ezekiel has a stunning encounter with the Son of Man, the Lord Jesus Himself, as he sits by the River Kebar in the land of the Babylonians:

> Spread out above the heads of the living creatures was what looked like an expanse, sparkling like ice, and awesome. Under the expanse their wings were stretched out one toward the other, and each had two wings covering its body. When the creatures moved, I heard the sound of their wings, like the roar of rushing waters, like the voice of the Almighty, like the tumult of an army. When they stood still, they lowered their wings. Then there came a voice from above the expanse over their heads as they stood with lowered wings. Above the expanse over their heads was what looked like a throne of sapphire, and high above on the throne was a figure like that of a man. I saw that from what appeared to be his waist up he looked like glowing metal, as if full of fire, and that from there down he looked like fire; and brilliant light surrounded him. Like the appearance of a rainbow in the clouds on a rainy day, so was the radiance around him. This was the appearance of the likeness of the glory of the LORD. When I saw it, I fell face down, and I heard the voice of one speaking. (Ezek. 1:22-28)

Wherever we are, no matter what we are facing, the real centre of life and truth is found in the unseen things that are known through Christ in the Spirit. There is a heaven where the Son of Man sits at the right hand of the Father, where the Holy Spirit directs a vast army of angels in the service of the church.

Isaiah opens by telling us of the many kings that came and went while he was preaching: Uzziah, Jotham, Ahaz and Hezekiah. He saw them come and go while preaching the gospel of Christ, the everlasting King. He would have experienced the disturbance of each of these political orders, but he was appointed to preach about the divine, righteous King who was and is and always will be. In the year that Uzziah died Isaiah saw the true King of heaven, high and exalted, and just the hem of His robe filled the temple (Isa. 6).

At times of crisis, facing exile or in exile, the prophets constantly lift the vision of the church and the world to these fundamental and eternal matters of life and death, seen from the perspective of heaven, the eternal Zion. The only real security, the only real life, is found in Christ and whether we live or die in the short-term crises, if we have Him then we have the eternal life that goes on into the heavenly Zion and then to the resurrection future.

The day of justice

The prophets thunder not only against Israel and Judah, but also against all the other nations of the world. The day of justice is for the whole world – just as the church is for the whole world. The earth is filled with the glory of Jesus and there can be no room for any of the shame, pride and sin of human kingdoms or religions:

> The mountains quake before him and the hills melt away.
> The earth trembles at his presence, the world and all who

live in it. Who can withstand his indignation? Who can endure his fierce anger? His wrath is poured out like fire; the rocks are shattered before him. The LORD is good, a refuge in times of trouble. He cares for those who trust in him, but with an overwhelming flood he will make an end of (Nineveh); he will pursue his foes into darkness. (Nahum 1:5-8)

Right now it may look as if the world is dominated by kingdoms and empires (multi-national corporations and media giants), yet they are nothing compared to the coming kingdom of the Son of Man. Right now it looks as if death is winning and life is losing; as if the cause of the humble is trampled under the feet of the arrogant and godless; as if the widow and the orphan have no hope of any life; as if the rich and violent get their own way; as if might is right and money makes the world go round. But a day is coming when all this will be put right, when the way of life will reign and the way of death will be thrown out forever:

You have wearied the LORD with your words. 'How have we wearied him?' you ask. By saying, 'All who do evil are good in the eyes of the LORD, and he is pleased with them' or 'Where is the God of justice?' 'See, I will send my messenger, who will prepare the way before me. Then suddenly the Lord you are seeking will come to his temple; the Messenger of the covenant, whom you desire, will come,' says the LORD Almighty. 'But who can endure the day of his coming? Who can stand when he appears? For he will be like a refiner's fire or a launderer's soap. He will sit as a refiner and purifier of silver; he will purify the Levites and refine them like gold and silver. Then the Lord will have men who will bring offerings in righteousness, and the offerings of Judah and Jerusalem will be acceptable to the Lord, as in days gone by, as in former years. So I will come near to you for judgment. I will be quick to testify against sorcerers, adulterers and perjurers, against those who defraud labourers of their wages, who oppress the widows and the fatherless, and deprive aliens of justice, but do not fear me,' says the Lord Almighty. (Mal. 2:17–3:5)

Warnings and previews

This mighty day of justice is coming on the whole world, but before it happens we see and experience many warnings and previews. In His great compassion and desire to bring all nations into the church, God brings samples of that final day of justice on the nations throughout history. He raises up one nation to pull down another, so that each will be warned that the kingdoms of this world, with all their arrogance and godlessness, must be torn down to make way for the final, everlasting kingdom of righteousness, goodness and love – the kingdom of the Lord Jesus Christ, the Son of Man.

Joel warns about the coming day of justice, yet he also warns how this day of justice will be previewed to Judah in the short term as invading armies destroy them:

Blow the trumpet in Zion; sound the alarm on my holy hill. Let all who live in the land tremble, for the day of the Lord is coming. It is close at hand – a day of darkness and gloom, a day of clouds and blackness. Like dawn spreading across the mountains a large and mighty army comes, such as never was of old nor ever will be in ages to come. Before them fire devours, behind them a flame blazes. Before them the land is like the garden of Eden, behind them, a desert waste – nothing escapes them. (Joel 2:1-3)

Isaiah shows us how the kingdoms of this world all fall under the judgment of Immanuel, the Anointed Servant. He knocks down all who stand in His way as His church goes out to all the peoples of the world.

Religion exposed

Sadly many people imagine they would like this day of justice to arrive because they mistakenly assume that they will be on the winning side when the righteous are vindicated. The prophets constantly pull down any false and flimsy delusions. The day of justice will expose the emptiness of human religion. Instead of religion we need to look for the true fruit of the Spirit – justice and righteousness; self-control and love; joy and patience.

> 'I hate, I despise your religious feasts; I cannot stand your assemblies. Even though you bring me burnt offerings and grain offerings, I will not accept them. Though you bring choice fellowship offerings, I will have no regard for them. Away with the noise of your songs! I will not listen to the music of your harps. But let justice roll on like a river, righteousness like a never-failing stream!' (Amos 5:21-24)

This is personal

Perhaps the most disturbing feature of the day of justice is the sheer anger of the Lord Almighty. This is not a dispassionate matter of sorting out legal infringements or enforcing a code of conduct. There is something deeply personal and passionate about the judgement that the LORD brings. When He summons the forces of Assyria to bring judgement on Judah, the LORD wants them to 'rejoice' in 'my triumph'. The language of wrath, fury and anger soaks through these descriptions of the day of justice:

> Raise a banner on a bare hilltop, shout to them; beckon to them to enter the gates of the nobles. I have commanded my holy ones; I have summoned my warriors to carry out my wrath – those who rejoice in my triumph. Listen, a noise on the mountains, like that of a great multitude! Listen, an uproar among the kingdoms, like nations massing together! The LORD Almighty is mustering an army for war. They come from faraway lands, from the ends of the heavens – the LORD and the weapons of his wrath – to destroy the whole country. Wail, for the day of the LORD is near; it will come like destruction from the Almighty. Because of this, all hands will go limp, every man's heart will melt. Terror will seize them, pain and anguish will grip them; they will writhe like a woman in labour. They will look aghast at each other, their faces aflame. See, the day of the LORD is coming – a cruel day, with wrath and fierce anger – to make the land desolate and destroy the sinners within it. (Isa. 13:2-9)

It is all too easy to lose this sense of the real anger of the living God against sin. I all too often surround myself with hymns, sermons and ideas of nothing but the compassion and love of God until in the end, due to the sinfulness of my heart and the darkened nature of my mind, I develop a twisted understanding of the Father, Son and Spirit. Without the corrective doctrine of these prophets I can lose sight of the cross of Jesus, the vileness of sin and the terror of the day of justice.

The divine warrior goes out

Though there are these preview days of judgement, yet there are times when the prophets look only to that final day of justice when the whole world is judged, that day when the Divine Warrior Himself will go out to war against all the forces of evil and darkness:

> See, the LORD is going to lay waste the earth and devastate it; he will ruin its face and scatter its inhabitants – it will be the same for priest as for people, for master as for servant, for mistress as for maid, for seller as for buyer, for borrower as for lender, for debtor as for creditor. The earth will be completely laid waste and totally plundered. The LORD has spoken this word. The earth dries up and withers, the world languishes and withers, the exalted of the earth languish. The earth is defiled by its people; they have disobeyed the laws, violated the statutes and broken the everlasting covenant. Therefore a curse consumes the earth; its people must bear their guilt. Therefore earth's inhabitants are burned up, and very few are left. (Isa. 24:1-6)

This world is going

Jesus told us that if we try to grasp on to this passing life we will lose our lives completely, but if we lose our lives in this age **for His sake** then we will actually find true life, both now and forever. These are deep words and challenge the basic instincts of this old mortal life.

The prophets had this same Spirit-inspired hope in the new creation that would flow out of the resurrection of the promised Messiah – for the transformation of the whole creation. They were given prophetic vision to see the King of all creation rising from the tomb and taking the whole heavens and the earth with Him into His eternal age of immortality:

> Behold, I will create new heavens and a new earth. The former things will not be remembered, nor will they come to mind. But be glad and rejoice forever in what I will create, for I will create Jerusalem to be a delight and its people a joy. I will rejoice over Jerusalem and take delight in my people; the sound of weeping and of crying will be heard in it no more. (Isa. 65:17-19)

Glen Scrivener explains Isaiah's point so well in his *King's English* meditations on Scripture: 'In a culture that says "Make the most of now", "Experience all you can", "There are no second chances" – Isaiah begs to differ. You don't need to see the Himalayas before you die. You can see them afterwards. You don't need to despair when your body stops working, it will start again. You can mourn your loved ones who have died in Christ, but you will hold them in your arms again. **This** body, **this** kind of life, **this** world will be raised, redeemed and renewed into even greater glory.'[1]

---

1. CTT Publishing, 2012.

Though the old Jerusalem of Isaiah's day was going to be destroyed in the judgements of exile, he was given the eyes to see another Jerusalem, of the heavens; a city with foundations that had a kind of resurrection life freed from all the pain and sorrow of the curse and death:[2]

> On this mountain the LORD Almighty will prepare a feast of rich food for all peoples, a banquet of aged wine – the best of meats and the finest of wines. On this mountain he will destroy the shroud that enfolds all peoples, the sheet that covers all nations; he will swallow up death forever. The Sovereign LORD will wipe away the tears from all faces; he will remove the disgrace of his people from all the earth. The LORD has spoken. In that day they will say, 'Surely this is our God; we trusted in him, and he saved us. This is the LORD, we trusted in him; let us rejoice and be glad in his salvation.' (Isa. 25:6-9)

Remember the curses of sin in Deuteronomy 28?

> You will be unsuccessful in everything you do; day after day you will be oppressed and robbed, with no one to rescue

---

2. Isaiah 65:20 has been the cause of great concern and speculation down the centuries! Some have even imagined that Jesus will do a half-hearted kind of restoration of the universe for a millennium before doing the job properly later on! However, this verse simply uses the ordinary language and phrases of human life. In John Newton's famous hymn 'Amazing Grace' he tries to get us to imagine the immortality of the new creation by writing 'When we've been there ten thousand years, Bright shining as the sun, We've no less days to sing God's praise, Than when we first begun.' In the same kind of way Isaiah asks us to imagine a world where being 100 years old will be considered as still being a youngster! This verse 'does not imply that death will still be present (contradicting 25:7-8) but rather affirms that over the whole of life, as we should now say from infancy to old age, the power of death will be destroyed' (Motyer, *The Prophecy of Isaiah*, page 530).

you. You will be pledged to be married to a woman, but another will take her and ravish her. You will build a house, but you will not live in it. You will plant a vineyard, but you will not even begin to enjoy its fruit. (Deut. 28:29-30)

In our resurrection future we will have houses and vineyards that belong to us that we will be able to enjoy for ourselves (Isa. 65:21-23). All the curses of sin will be gone forever. The LORD will be so near and so attentive to His pure and righteous people that He will respond before they have finished asking (v. 24).

They will build houses and dwell in them; they will plant vineyards and eat their fruit. No longer will they build houses and others live in them, or plant and others eat. For as the days of a tree, so will be the days of my people; my chosen ones will long enjoy the works of their hands. They will not toil in vain or bear children doomed to misfortune; for they will be a people blessed by the LORD, they and their descendants with them. Before they call I will answer; while they are still speaking I will hear. (Isa. 65:21-24)

Again we are reminded this redemption is not just for human beings, but for the whole creation – including the animals.

The wolf and the lamb will feed together, and the lion will eat straw like the ox, but dust will be the serpent's food. 'They will neither harm nor destroy on all my holy mountain,' says the LORD. (Isa. 65:25)

The wedding day of Christ and the church

The LORD's day of justice and vengeance is at the same time His great day of resurrection and new creation. In fact that

147

great day of destruction and restoration will actually be the wedding day of Christ and the church. Isaiah 62 clearly describes how the church is the bride of the Lord and the land itself will be restored as the marriage home.

> No longer will they call you Deserted, or name your land Desolate. But you will be called Hephzibah, and your land Beulah; for the Lord will take delight in you, and your land will be married. As a young man marries a maiden, so will your sons marry you; as a bridegroom rejoices over his bride, so will your God rejoice over you. (Isa. 62:4-5)

Isaiah 63 shows us the divine bridegroom going out to prepare the family home, driving out all that is evil and godless, as He works that terrifying work alone sustained by His own anger and passion. On that day He will first judge the world, pouring out His divine wrath on all the wicked to take them away for ever. Yet, this judgment is done to prepare the heavens and the earth to be redeemed and reordered as the everlasting home of righteousness.

Gathering it all together

The final chapter of Isaiah gathers all these themes together. The people of Isaiah's day needed to know that the temple in Jerusalem was not the most important thing. It would be destroyed when they were taken into exile and would be finished once for all after Christ had completed His work. So, the Lord declares that if heaven is His throne and earth is His footstool what kind of temple could any of us possibly build for Him? (66:1).

Within Israel (vv. 5-6) there is deep division between those who genuinely tremble at the word of God and those who mock it. The mockers hated those who loved the LORD, as if they said, 'You are always going on about the glory of Christ! The only thing that seems to make you joyful is the LORD's glory. Let's see this glory so that you can finally have your strange joy!' The LORD promises that even though those people are perhaps genetically children of Abraham, there is nothing for them but death and destruction (v. 6).

The LORD describes Zion as producing many children – an idea that He has set before us many times throughout the book. She will give birth to all her children with no labour pains. In fact she will give birth in a moment, a whole nation in a day (vv. 7-13).[3]

The Lord is coming. To the church that thought makes our hearts rejoice, but His enemies must face His fury (vv. 14-15). The Lord is coming with fire to purge the world. He comes with His furious anger and with flames of fire to destroy all the wicked with their pagan worship and disregard for the law of the LORD (vv. 15-17).

---

3. '...this was a figure of the setting up of the Christian Church in the world, and the replenishing of that family with children which was to be named from Jesus Christ. When the Spirit was poured out, and the gospel went forth from Zion, multitudes were converted in a little time and with little pains compared with the vast product. The apostles, even before they travailed, brought forth, and the children born to Christ were so numerous, and so suddenly and easily produced, that they were rather like the dew from the morning's womb than like the son from the mother's womb, Ps. cx. 3. The success of the gospel was astonishing; that light, like the morning, strangely diffused itself till it took hold even of the ends of the earth. Cities and nations were born at once to Christ. The same day that the Spirit was poured out there were 3000 souls added to the Church. And, when this glorious work was once begun, it was carried on wonderfully, beyond what could be imagined, so mightily grew the word of God and prevailed' (Matthew Henry, 'Matthew Henry's commentary on the whole Bible: complete and unabridged in one volume', Peabody: Hendrickson. [1994], p. 1216).

Christ's glory must first be displayed to all the nations (vv. 18-21). People of every nation and language (v. 18) will see His glory – from as far away as Tarshish in Spain or Libya in North Africa or Greece or even more distant islands like Great Britain or Australia or Indonesia or Japan (v. 19). The church will find brothers in all the nations of the world, just as Psalm 87 said (v. 20). Those Gentiles will be so completely joined to the church that they could even serve as Aaronic or Levitical priests at the temple.

The new heavens and the new earth are our true home: a home that will last forever and ever (v. 22). This old form of the universe is decaying and wearing out, but that resurrection age will never wear out. All humanity will be part of that new creation, yet those who refused and rebelled will have no future there at all. Whereas the righteous have immortal bodies, the bodies of the wicked, having been destroyed by the LORD with His furious anger, will be left to be eaten by the worms – worms who will never be satisfied. However arrogant the wicked might be in this passing age, when Christ comes they will have no honour at all. In fact, all that will be left will be 'loathsome to all mankind' (v. 24).

In the end, when all has been put right, the vain glory and shame of evil and darkness will finally be thrown away into the rubbish tip of the outer darkness forever and ever. The glory of the LORD Jesus Christ will finally be unrivalled, filling the whole creation. Christ and His bride will enjoy that new creation forever and ever, revelling in the eternal life of God free from the dangers of sin and evil once and for all:

And I saw a new heaven and a new earth: for the first heaven and the first earth were passed away; and there was no more sea. And I John saw the holy city, new Jerusalem, coming down from God out of heaven, prepared as a bride adorned for her husband. And I heard a great voice out of heaven saying, Behold, the tabernacle of God is with men, and he will dwell with them, and they shall be his people, and God himself shall be with them, and be their God. And God shall wipe away all tears from their eyes; and there shall be no more death, neither sorrow, nor crying, neither shall there be any more pain: for the former things are passed away. And he that sat upon the throne said, Behold, I make all things new. (Rev. 21:1-5 KJV)

CHAPTER 7

THE WAY OF THE RIGHTEOUS OR THE WICKED

EVERYBODY, whether openly or secretly, has deep feelings about their own mortality. Is this the end of existence or is there another world beyond death? How can we know for sure? Is it all in the end just wishful thinking and groundless speculation?

The wisdom literature of the Bible takes us right into the personal experience of living as followers of Jesus Christ. As we think about heaven and hell, life and death, we feel these things very deeply.

Some strange theories!

It is good to remind ourselves as we begin of the radical difference between the Biblical teaching about heaven and hell on the one hand and the Greek theory of the 'immortality of the soul' on the other.

The ancient Greeks had all kinds of odd ideas about the human body and the survival of an invisible component called the soul or spirit. They usually took the view that the body was inferior to the mind, so Plato imagined that the perishable body was sustained by an imperishable soul.[1]

The Bible has no time for this kind of abstract theory about the essence of the soul. Whatever life we have is totally determined by our relationship to Jesus, the life and light of the world. In His presence there is paradise. Apart from Him there is only darkness, chaos and death. God alone is immortal and He shares that immortality, through the resurrection of Jesus, with His church.

Whatever lifeless and tormented existence anything or anybody has in hell, eternal isolation from Jesus is hardly worthy of the name 'immortality'.[2]

---

1. He also had a strange idea that we could 'remember' truth learned before we were born. Plato believed that because our invisible souls were part of the eternal form of life, therefore they could not die. Another Greek view, drawn from that same pagan world of thought, was that anything that was simple – that is, just one thing without any parts – could not perish because it could not be broken down into anything smaller. So, if the soul is a simple thing then it must be immortal.

2. Other views have been put forward throughout the world. Some have argued that there is a principle of life within us that endures beyond the death of our body, but that it takes on another form after we die. Thus, we might return to life as an animal of some kind or perhaps a human at another social level than before. Others have taken the view that the human soul or spirit or 'ghost' goes on to some realm to live with the ancestors or the great heroes of the past. The northern European pagans tended to believe that those who were brave and worthy warriors would be allowed to join the feasting hall of Odin and Thor in Valhalla. Versions of this are replicated all over the world in different ways. Some think that the human spirit is finally united with the

We cannot talk of 'immortality' going on in hell. Existence in hell is lifeless, empty and meaningless. It is the very opposite of the true immortality of the living God.

In more modern thinking the idea is that we 'live on' in the memories of those who are still alive. Unless we achieve great fame or notoriety our 'existence' beyond death will not last more than a generation or so at best! Sometimes this is changed into the idea of 'living on' genetically in our children and grandchildren, giving no continued existence at all to those who produce no offspring. This kind of 'ancestor worship' has been very popular in many mythologies around the world throughout history.

People often assume that the teaching of the Bible is in some way connected to this confusion of theories. But the Bible has none of these small-scale theories to account for life beyond death. Everything in the Bible is related to the Lord Jesus Christ as the life and logic of the whole creation.

Taken by the angels to be with Him in paradise at death, the church awaits the final day when heaven and earth will be reunited as the everlasting solid home of righteousness. The way of Jesus, mapped out from Genesis to Revelation, is of a total renewal of the entire universe where all His people live fully physical lives in **this** renewed physical world forever and ever. His people will live physical lives with Him and the Father in the fullness of the Spirit forever and ever.

'world spirit'. There are no end of these imaginative ideas, but if humanity rejects or ignores the truth in Jesus then why not pursue these fanciful and speculative theories? To try to argue that one is more 'rational' than another is truly a fool's errand!

The Bible has no interest in theories of immortality of the soul or even mere *theories* of resurrection or reincarnation. From beginning to end, its attention is fixed only on the resurrection hope of Christ Himself.

Resurrection hope – from the earliest of times

In the wisdom literature as a whole we find, in what is perhaps the very earliest book of the whole Bible, an extremely clear and certain resurrection hope in Christ in the Book of Job:

> Oh, that my words were recorded,
> that they were written on a scroll,
> that they were inscribed with an iron tool on lead,
> or engraved in rock forever!
> I know that my Redeemer lives,
> and that in the end he will stand on the earth.
> And after my skin has been destroyed,
> yet in my flesh I will see God;
> I myself will see him
> with my own eyes – I, and not another.
> How my heart yearns within me!
>
> (Job 19:23-27)

Think of Job's life. He had a wonderful family and a dream home. All was going well for him – and then it was all taken away. His friends could offer him no real comfort. It seemed he had nothing left, no reason left to live. Yet, in the depths of his anguish he goes back to the one thing that could never be taken away from him: his Redeemer, Christ standing at the Father's side.

Remember that Job probably lived around 1800 B.C., perhaps 300 years before Moses wrote the Pentateuch, when Stonehenge was being built in Britain. When others were descending into the depths of paganism, Job held on to his resurrection hope in Christ the Redeemer. He wanted his words to be remembered forever, and here we are still studying those words today.

Job knew that his Redeemer would 'in the end' stand on the earth. Like Enoch, he had a great focus on that final day of resurrection and judgement. His life had been redeemed by Christ. Even after his body had decayed away, he knew it would one day be reconstituted by Christ's resurrection power.

In his flesh he would see God.

> I **myself** will see him
> with **my own** eyes – **I**, and not another.

Christ the centre and soul of the psalms

The book of Psalms is far more than a record of the feelings of ancient songwriters. It is a record of the inner life of Christ Himself and His people. He leads the church in prayer and worship, so we can pray His prayers in Him.

Obviously Jesus Christ is the default speaker in the psalms. He alone is the Blessed Man; the Man at the LORD's right hand; the Man with clean hands and a pure heart; the Man who can ask to be judged according to His own righteousness; the divine King before whom the nations cower; the One against whom rebellious humanity plots.

Yet, there are some psalms where Christ's people come into the foreground, as we look to Him to take away our sin and cleanse us from our transgressions.

The key point is that Christ is the centre and soul of the psalms. He shows us how to think and feel about all the issues of life, death and eternity. Through His prophets like David, Asaph and the sons of Korah, Jesus Christ ensures that **His own thoughts of life, death, resurrection and ascension** are explored and described in all their emotional intensity.

How to teach ourselves His truth

Some of the most powerful psalms show us how Jesus faced death. Even though He felt almost overwhelmed with grief as He faced His God-forsaken death, He shows us how to control our thoughts and continue to trust in God even in the hardest and darkest of times.

As we look at the themes of heaven and hell, death and paradise, judgement day and new creation in the psalms, we find anxieties about death; concerns that the wicked will get away with their evil; fears that the righteous will fall; concerns that the LORD God has forgotten His people or no longer does the amazing things that He used to do. There are even cries from the depths when we fear that we are not saved at all, that we are falling into death and hell.

The book takes us into this prayer life of Jesus, and in this chapter we see especially how it takes us into the issues of life and death, heaven and hell that Jesus faced particularly in that final testing.

All these concerns and deep emotions are the genuine experience of Christ and the Church in this present darkness. We know the truth and we continue to drum the truth of God's word in at the deepest level. Yet, our emotions, through the tiredness, stresses, illnesses, failings and conflicts of this life, do not always conform to the truth in Jesus. Through the psalms, Christ shows us how to confront or deal with these fears and anxieties, how to teach ourselves His truth when the Abyss tries to overwhelm us.

On the other hand, we find the hopes, joy and praise of Christ and His saints as they express confidence in the face of death; reassurance at the certainty of the final day; profound explorations of the death, resurrection and ascension of Jesus Christ and all the way through a focus on the City of God, the holy Mountain of paradise, Zion itself as the true and final home of the Church, whether after death awaiting the new creation or at the very end when the City of God descends to the renewed earth forevermore.

A stark choice

The opening psalm sets before us the stark choice between life or death, Christ or the wicked, the Blessed Man or sinners.

On the one hand there is life (like Eden) with the tree planted by that vibrant river, bearing its fruit and never suffering any withering or decay. The Blessed Man Christ delights in the LORD. He is obsessed with the word of God night and day.

Often this psalm is explained as if it was just advising us on how to live our lives. In extreme examples the wording is changed from 'Blessed is the Man' to 'Blessed are those who' – as if it were advice to people in general! However, this psalm is deliberately a contrast between the one Man and the many wicked. It is about the only way to truly **live**. There is only ever one way to **live**. Jesus' life runs on through death into paradise and the new creation. If we have His life then we live, but if we do not then we wither and die. The psalm gives us hope if we see Him as our life, our champion: His people do 'not wither', forever and ever.

Christ's life is starkly contrasted with the wicked. They take counsel together in their sin as they mock Christ (v. 1). For all their arrogance, they are nothing but chaff. Their life has no substance and death really does take them away. The Spirit blows them away in a moment. On the day of judgement they will be unable to stand. There will be no place for the wicked in the assembly of the righteous of the new creation. There is no place for them in Christ's future.

The Righteous Man (and His people) is the focus of attention for the Living God. He **knows** the righteous. The wicked simply perish.

If we are going to understand heaven and hell in the psalms we have to do more than simply look for occurrences of the words 'heaven' and 'hell'![3] Eternal life begins right

---

3. In recent years there have been infamous attempts to re-think or re-imagine heaven and hell. One claimed to have carefully studied every occurrence of the words 'heaven' and 'hell' – yet the Bible's teaching about our eternal future goes far beyond those specific words. These recent revisions of heaven and hell are disappointing because they typically refuse to engage with the constantly repeated language of the punishment of the wicked throughout the Bible. The language of heaven is taken far more literally than the language of hell and destruction, even to the point that hell ends up being almost an expression of God's love as a kind of remedial correction centre that anyone can leave at any time once they have reformed. The contrast with C.S. Lewis in *The Great Divorce* is interesting. Lewis does not attack the classic Biblical teaching about hell, but rather he is trying to defend it against the idea that all roads finally lead to heaven. On the title page Lewis quotes from George MacDonald that there can be no compromise between heaven and hell, that Satan must be cast out 'every hair and feather'. Lewis tries to explore the psychology of heaven versus the psychology of hell, showing how desperately divided they are and how utterly narrow, closed, self-destructive and insubstantial the people in hell really are. David Wayne says of Lewis's depiction, 'Hell is a place of unreality, where the souls of the damned wander around,

here and now as soon as a person begins to trust and follow Jesus, the Blessed and Righteous Man, the LORD's Anointed.

As we have seen, hell is simply the final home for sin. It is alienation from God. It begins right here and now when we live in the darkness and serve the cravings of our deceitful desires. The wicked live in deceitful plots and traps, greed and violence, all of which will finally come back on them. On the day of God there will be no place for them except in the destruction and perishing of that final, endless ruin.

The life of praising and serving God that we begin right here and now goes on forever and ever, on to that resurrection future at the renewal of all things.

Eternal life begins now and rises up to an everlasting future – and eternal death begins now and falls away into an everlasting future.

Rebellion and destruction of the wicked

The rebellion and destruction of the wicked are taken up in more detail in Psalm 2. In Psalm 1:1 they take counsel together in their mocking sin, but in Psalm 2 it has become a global plot, headed up by world leaders, against the Father and Christ the King.[4]

This conspiracy of rebellion and defiance against Christ might seem strong from earth, but from the City of God it is simply laughable (v. 4). The whole earth is the final

---

forever bound to their sinful desires and forever doomed to frustration in their attempts to fulfill their desires' (The blog of David Wayne, the pastor of Grace Point Presbyterian Church in Severn, MD. http://jollyblogger. typepad.com/jollyblogger/2005/04/review of the g.html).

4. How strange it is that the translators typically translate Psalm 2:2 as 'Anointed One' rather than 'Christ'!

inheritance of Christ (v. 8) and the wicked rebellion has as much chance as a china tea cup meeting an iron bar at great speed. There is a day coming when the anger of the Son (v. 12) will flare up and all those who are against Him will be destroyed. On the other hand, those who take refuge in Him will be 'blessed'.

That final sentence in Psalm 2 is vital. Jesus Christ is the Blessed Man. His blessed and everlasting life is available for all who will take refuge in Him. He has been installed in Zion, God's holy mountain. The hope of the saints is to go to that City of God where the river of life is beyond the reach of death or Sheol.

If we have taken refuge in Christ the Son then we too are blessed. Our home is His home; our life His life; our future His future. The wicked like chaff or broken pottery must simply be thrown away.

The testing time of night

Psalm 3 introduces a common theme in the psalms: the testing time of night.

We know that Jesus saw a clear connection between sleep and death. He describes Jairus' daughter as 'sleeping' when she was clearly dead and raised her to life as if she were just sleeping (Matt. 9:18-26)!

As the LORD of life, Jesus is able to wake His people from death as easily as we might wake someone from sleep. In fact, He created us in such a way that every day we have an experience of death and resurrection. Every night we fall into death, but every morning we experience the resurrection of waking up! He wanted us to have many trial runs at death so that we would easily trust Him when it comes to that final sleep of this mortal body.

Some of us might not **feel** as if we have been resurrected very well in the morning – at least not until we have had a cup of coffee – but nevertheless the pattern of sleeping/waking is fundamental to all human life. Studies show that if we are deprived of sleep for around two weeks we simply die – almost as if our bodies simply cannot cope without an experience of death and resurrection and would prefer to die completely rather than go on in that way.

We find this same thought in the Book of Common Prayer. We pray, 'Accept this our morning sacrifice of praise and thanksgiving; for His sake who lay down in the grave, and rose again for us, Your Son our Saviour Jesus Christ.'

So, as we see these references to sleeping peacefully and safely awaking in the morning, it is good for us to look more closely. Yes, there is advice about getting a good night's sleep, but it is usually quite clear that we are really thinking about that final sleep and the waking up of resurrection morning.

Our resurrection hope

Psalm 3 is a prophecy of Jesus facing death. Jesus felt very isolated as His enemies surrounded Him on the cross. Yet, He could commit His spirit into the Father's hands, leaving His body also in the Father's safe keeping, knowing His dead body would be woken up on the third day:

> To the LORD I cry aloud, and he answers me from his holy hill (v. 4).

> I lie down and sleep; I wake again, because the LORD sustains me (v. 5).

163

Matthew Henry comments on this that the one who trusts in Christ 'is very secure, because God Himself has undertaken to keep him safe. When he comes to sleep the sleep of death, and to lie down in the grave, and to make his bed in the darkness, he will then, with good old Simeon, depart in peace (Luke 2:29), being assured that God will receive his soul, to be safe with Himself, and that his body also shall be made to dwell in safety in the grave.'[5]

Our resurrection hope is reflected in the way we go to sleep each night. Every night we are given a chance to prepare for the day of our death. Every morning we can deepen our trust in Jesus with His renewed grace.

Sleepless nights

In Psalm 6 there can be no sleep at night because there is a terrifying fear of death. The fear of being abandoned or falling into Sheol or hell is so overwhelming there can only be sleepless nights of tears.

Until our hearts are settled about the matter of heaven and hell, we are always in danger of sleepless nights.

Certain knowledge that evil will be dealt with

In Psalm 5 there is confident praise in the morning. Why? Why did David and Christ get such a good night's sleep? Why are they filled with such resurrection hope and joy?

It might seem odd but the joy comes from the certain knowledge that evil and the wicked will have no sanctuary on the day of God. The wicked cannot dwell with Him. They will be

---

5. Matthew Henry, 'Matthew Henry's commentary on the whole Bible: complete and unabridged in one volume', Peabody: Hendrickson. [1994], p. 749.

thrown out of the heavens and the earth into that outer rubbish tip of darkness. In fact, God **hates** all who do wrong (v. 5), will destroy liars (v. 6) and **abhors** deceitful and bloodthirsty people.

As we look at the world and see the apparent victory of evil, how can we face death and the future with peace or confidence?

The surface view in this present darkness is that evil will triumph and death will have the final word. So many anti-Christian websites link to pictures and videos that revel in death, brutality, suffering and apparently random tragedy. They are deliberately preaching a message of darkness and meaninglessness. This is the attack on Christ and His people that is faced here and in so many psalms.

There is no place for violence, evil and wickedness with God. He hates it all and will destroy it. In verse 10 the psalm asks the Lord to 'banish them for their many sins'. Hell is real. It was designed for the destruction of the wicked. The reality of judgement day brings great comfort.

For ever and ever

Psalm 9 is a deep psalm that was sung to the tune 'The Death of the Son'. If God the Son has been killed, we might imagine this would be a psalm of great sorrow and yet it is the very opposite. It is a song of great triumph and victory because the death of the Son is the true defeat of death and hell:

> I will praise you, O Lord, with all my heart;
> I will tell of all your wonders.
> I will be glad and rejoice in you;
> I will sing praise to your name, O Most High.
>
> (vv. 1-2)

The wicked have been defeated, and their destruction is permanent. Verses 5-6 emphasise that the judgement and destruction against them is forever and ever. Some might suggest that hell is temporary and that it is possible to return from this judgement but it is hard to fit that teaching in with this psalm.

> You have rebuked the nations and destroyed the wicked;
> you have blotted out their name **for ever and ever**.
> **Endless** ruin has overtaken the enemy,
> you have uprooted their cities;
> **even the memory of them has perished**.

The most terrible words of judgement Jesus will speak on that final day will be 'I never knew you'. Here we are told that they will never be **remembered** either.

Lifted up from death

When we die, if we are trusting Christ we cannot be dragged down to the grave or Sheol. Our hope, through Christ, is to go up to the dwelling of God while we wait for the resurrection of all things.

> Have mercy and lift me up from the gates of death,
> that I may declare your praises
> in the gates of the Daughter of Zion
> and there rejoice in your salvation. (Ps. 9:13-14)

As we die, we will not really *die* but we will be taken up to Zion and continue praising and enjoying the fellowship of the living God in His presence.

I was reading about the final words of a missionary who had spent a long life working in China. He turned to those around his bed and simply said, 'If we live the eternal life now, we will always.'

That is what we find throughout the psalms. If we are worshipping the LORD right now, thirsting for Him, loving Him, enjoying His presence, then that is what we will do forever and ever in His presence. Of course, if we are not known to Him now and we are still cowering in the darkness clinging onto our selfish and deceitful desires, then that is all we will ever know now and forever.

A vivid picture of the future

In Psalm 11 we find a vivid picture of the future:

> The LORD is in his holy temple;
> the LORD is on his heavenly throne.
> He observes the sons of men;
> his eyes examine them.
> The LORD examines the righteous,
> but the wicked and those who love violence
> his soul hates.
> On the wicked he will rain
> fiery coals and burning sulphur;
> a scorching wind will be their lot.
> For the LORD is righteous,
> he loves justice;
> upright men **will see his face**.
>
> (vv. 4-7)

These verses recall the imagery of hell from the destruction of Sodom and Gomorrah, with the fiery coals and burning sulphur. Under such intense heat, exposed to scorching wind, the thirst is unbearable. The rain is burning sulphur rather than refreshing water. There is no satisfaction in hell, just a continual craving for more things that can never satisfy – that unwanted gnawing hunger and thirst for the Living God who has closed the door forever.

The upright gaze on the Father's face and are utterly satisfied. We were created in the image of God, created to share that life and fellowship of the Father, Son and Holy Spirit. When we know even as we are known, when we see face to face, we will be what we were made for.

God hates the wicked

In our postmodern culture it is all too easy to think of God as nothing but love – or to define His love in such a way that there is no place for His passion or holiness or righteousness. Our culture is comfortable with a God who loves **everybody** all the time without any judgement or condemnation. Romans 8:1 says that there is no condemnation **for those who are in Christ Jesus**, but some of the religious thought of our day says that there is no condemnation for **anybody** – whether they are in Jesus or not.

When we really get into these psalms perhaps the most shocking thing about them is the genuine anger and hatred God has for sinful humanity. I'm so used to the truth that God **loves** the world that I almost forget that He hates the wicked:

> You are not a God who takes pleasure in evil… you hate all who do wrong. (Ps. 5:4-5)

God is a righteous judge, a God who expresses his wrath
every day.
(Ps. 7:11)

The wicked and those who love violence his soul hates.
(Ps. 11:5)

If we do not take this seriously we cannot understand why the
psalms are so full of destruction and ruin. The predicament of
the human race is so much more serious than we ever dream.
We are born as willing and eager troops in a war against
God that has been going on for thousands of years. We fight
among ourselves and in futile fury we throw ourselves against
the Rock of Ages until finally we are crushed by Him. Yet,
in all this darkness and chaos, that Rock of Ages gave His
life so that whoever trusts in Him would not perish but have
eternal life.

To betray or ignore **that** love and holiness, that righteousness and mercy, is terrible. The superior army is marching
against us and the divine general has provided a way of
peace, at enormous personal cost. If we refuse that offer
and try to hole up in the tower we have built, then there
can be nothing but destruction and ruin when He finally
arrives.

How then can we get to heaven?

If our great hope is to live with LORD on His holy hill, in His
sanctuary, to gaze on His face and delight in Him, how can
we ever get there?

It is in Psalm 16 that we are taken right to the heart of the
resurrection hope of the whole Bible. This is the very passage
Peter preached from on the Day of Pentecost in Acts 2:

I have set the LORD always before me.
Because he is at my right hand,
I will not be shaken.
Therefore my heart is glad and my tongue rejoices;
my body also will rest secure,
because you will not abandon me to the grave,
nor will you let your Holy One see decay.
You have made known to me the path of life;
you will fill me with joy in your presence,
with eternal pleasures at your right hand. (Ps. 16:8-11)

Jesus knew He could not be shaken even when He faced His God-forsaken and cursed death. He knew that death and Sheol would not hold on to Him and His body would not even be allowed to decay in the grave.

Christ is on the path of life. As we follow Him we start walking on that path right now. The path keeps going on into eternal life regardless of the fact that it passes through the valley of the **shadow** of death. Then in the presence of God Himself we have 'eternal pleasures at his right hand'.

The wicked cannot see beyond death. They may have myths and fantasies about some kind of 'life after death' but Christ's resurrection means nothing to them. Any treasure they acquire, any glory they enjoy, is only for now. As Jesus simply says in Matthew 6:2 and 5, they have 'received their reward in full'.

Though in this life the righteous have many troubles, we have hope – 'In righteousness I shall see your face; when I awake, I shall be satisfied with seeing your likeness.' (Ps. 17:15)

Doesn't this remind us so much of the resurrection hope of Job? Job knew that he would see God in his own flesh, with his own eyes, on resurrection morning – waking up to the face of the Father.

Sheol with its shadowy, lifeless darkness is the default destination for the human race at death, yet by His death and resurrection Christ has opened the way to eternal life for ever.

> He asked you for life, and you gave it to him –
> **length of days, for ever and ever**.
> Through the victories you gave, his glory is great;
> you have bestowed on him splendour and majesty.
> Surely you have granted him **eternal blessings**
> and made him glad with the joy of your presence.
> For the King trusts in the LORD;
> through the unfailing love of the Most High
> **he will not be shaken**.
>   (Ps. 21:4-7)

No place for the wicked

There is no place for the wicked on the earth.

The future of the wicked is destruction, ruin and death no matter how prosperous and successful they seem to be right now. In opposing God, in pursuing evil and sin, they have left the path of life and are on that broad way of death that keeps on going into hell forever and ever. There is no place for the wicked in the LORD's presence or in His renewed creation.

In Psalm 101 Christ ensures that the wicked are excluded from His house, cut off from the LORD's city:

> My eyes will be on the faithful in the land,
> that they may dwell with me;
> he whose walk is blameless
> will minister to me.
> No one who practises deceit
> will dwell in my house;
> no one who speaks falsely
> will stand in my presence.
> Every morning I will put to silence
> all the wicked in the land;
> I will cut off every evildoer
> from the city of the LORD. (vv. 6-8)

The wicked will see all the good things of the blessed man in Psalm 112: (v. 10) 'The wicked man will see and be vexed; he will gnash his teeth and waste away; the longings of the wicked will come to nothing.'

When Jesus speaks of the wicked gnashing their teeth as they are thrown into the outer darkness of hell on that last day, this may well be the psalm He has in mind. The wicked resent the blessings of Christ and His people, because all their own desires can never satisfy.

The fountain of life

We face many troubles and death itself, yet we remain unshaken. We look forward to our bodies being woken up on that final day of resurrection when Christ takes His inheritance and shares it all with His people, His body and bride.

Psalm 36 states this hope in wonderful terms:

> How priceless is your unfailing love!
> Both high and low among men
> find refuge in the shadow of your wings.
> They feast on the abundance of your house;
> you give them drink from your river of delights.
> For **with you is the fountain of life**;
> in your light we see light. (vv. 7-9)

Those who have made the LORD their dwelling-place look forward to the morning when we will be satisfied. We can sing for joy and are glad all our days because if the favour of the LORD is on us we can be 'established'. We can live the 'long life' of eternal life with the LORD – for ever and ever.[6]

> You guide me with your counsel,
> and **afterward you will take me into glory**.
> Whom have I in heaven but you?
> And earth has nothing I desire besides you.
> My flesh and my heart may fail,
> but God is the strength of my heart
> and my portion forever.
>
> (Ps. 73:24-26)

---

6. We see this with the fifth commandment – 'Honour your father and your mother, so that you may live long in the land the LORD your God is giving you.' As Paul explains in Ephesians 6, this means that parents must bring up their children **in the LORD**, teaching their children to trust in Jesus on the path of life leading to heaven and the new creation. Long life in the Bible means so much more than living to be 100! It means living eternal life, everlasting life.

CHAPTER 8

THE WINNOWING FORK

WHEN Jesus speaks about our life beyond death He states simple promises that take our breath away, promises that seem utterly impossible.

In John 8:51 He says, 'Very truly I tell you, whoever obeys my word **will never see death.**'

In John 11:26 He promises that 'whoever lives by believing in me **will never die.**'

We might assume that this life He gives must refer to some life in another world or life after the resurrection of the future, but He also states very plainly in John 5:24-25, 'Very truly I tell you, whoever hears my word and believes him who sent me has eternal life and will not be judged but has crossed over from death to life. Very truly I tell you, a time is coming **and has now come** when the dead will hear the voice of the Son of God and those who hear will live.'

In other words Jesus not only promises that life will be given to dead bodies on the day of resurrection in the future (John 5:28-29) but that right now life will be given to anybody who trusts Him – and this life from Jesus cannot ever be overcome by death. If we have life from Jesus we will never die or ever see death.

At face value these promises seem to go too far! We have seen many Christians die. Or have we? We have seen the **bodies** of many Christians die, but is there more to this situation than meets the eye?

What does Jesus mean by life and death?

Just how powerful is the Lord Jesus?

When we come to Jesus Himself on the subject of heaven and hell we step into a different atmosphere. Everybody else in the Bible speaks about the day of judgement as a witness. The prophets and the apostles tell us what God is going to do with the wicked and the righteous both now and forever; but when we listen to Jesus Himself the change in focus is so striking it is deeply unnerving. He speaks as the one who will throw people into hell; the one who will resurrect the dead; the one who will divide up the human race into righteous and wicked; the one who will judge the world with total power and justice.

There is a strange calm and authority throughout Jesus' words about the day when He comes in great glory to judge the world.

He will divide the wicked from the righteous

With no arrogance or pride, Jesus constantly and with total assurance of truth and justice describes how He will divide out and eternally separate the wicked from the righteous, the goats from the sheep; darkness from light; death from life. He knows what He is going to do on that day and He speaks about His future words and actions as if they have already happened. There is no hysteria or angst, no sense of stress or pressure. He tells us that He will throw into the outer darkness anyone that He does not know – and they will be left weeping and gnashing their teeth in their anger and hatred against Him.

The fact that they will rage at Him with hate for all eternity does not intimidate Him or drive Him to compromise. He is utterly calm and assured in who He is and what He will do.

Jesus not only describes how He will speak and act at the end of the age but He also demonstrates right there and then that He can raise the dead with a word, feed the hungry with plenty to spare, drive out demons, command nature and cure every disease of body and mind. When He tells us what He is going to do, we know He is speaking the truth.

The other stark fact is that Jesus speaks more directly and deliberately about the fate of the wicked than anyone else. In fact He spends more time warning of that future rejection than He does describing the joys of the new creation.

He has comparatively little to say about the marriage feast of the Lamb or the 'renewal of all things' compared to what He says about the experience of the unprepared, the unbelieving and the unfruitful on the day when He suddenly returns to winnow the world – to sift out the chaff and burn it in the fire.

Everything that's gone before...

As we have seen, Jesus Christ is the light, life and order of the whole creation. Without Him there is only chaos and emptiness. With the flood He took the wicked away to begin again with a kind of 'new creation'. He left Sodom and Gomorrah in smoking ruins as a witness of the final judgement to come. He judged Egypt and showed what it means to be shut off from Him – disease, darkness, emptiness, ruin and death. In the former prophets we saw how the day of judgement will mean the total destruction of all wickedness, so that the righteous may inherit the earth under His reign. In the psalms we read there is no future for the wicked at all and God will remember them no more when He has thrown them out in that final day.

In His presence there is life and light, food and water, purpose and fruitfulness, and fellowship with the Father in His Spirit.

We need to keep all this in mind when we read the gospels. It is all vital. The light of the Old Testament explains what is going on in the life and teaching of Jesus of Nazareth.

The Old Testament illumines the New Testament. We cannot understand the New Testament without the Old Testament. On their own, the New Testament Scriptures are like an isolated chapter of a book where we don't know the characters, the story line, the heroes or villains.

The end of life as we know it

When Matthew begins his biography of Jesus by taking us back through His genealogy, he is reminding us that Jesus is the divine King who will end the exile from the living God. When he quotes Isaiah 7:14 in 1:22-23 he is telling us that Jesus is nothing less than the Living God living on earth. If there can be no death or sin, disease or devils in the presence of God, then the presence of Jesus can only mean the end of the world as we know it. If God is determined to live here on earth, making His eternal home right here among us, then nothing can remain as it is right now. There is a desperate need for a sorting out, a sifting, a division, a cleansing, a shaking of all things, a day when all that is wrong will be judged and removed. If sin, sickness, sorrow and sighing are all excluded from the life of God, and if God is going to be with us forever and ever, the day of judgement is the number one item on the world's agenda.

So, when John the Baptist introduces the world to Jesus, his words are deeply disturbing for this whole world order:

> The axe is already at the root of the trees, and every tree that does not produce good fruit will be cut down and thrown into the fire. I baptize you with water for repentance. But after me will come one who is more powerful than I, whose sandals I am not fit to carry. He will baptize you with the Holy Spirit and with fire. His winnowing fork is in his hand, and he will clear his threshing floor, gathering his wheat into his barn and burning up the chaff with unquenchable fire. (Matt. 3:10-12)

Stop for a moment to consider those words.

John the Baptist is the greatest of all the prophets and he introduces Jesus as the One who is coming to 'clean house'. He is coming to get rid of all the rubbish and throw it out on to the bonfire. He describes Jesus as having an axe in one hand and a tool for separating wheat from chaff in the other. He comes with fire. John was able to ceremonially wash the people with mere water to **symbolically** cleanse them, but Jesus would truly cleanse with fire and the Spirit. Notice that whereas His wheat would be gathered safely into His barn, yet the chaff would be burned with 'unquenchable fire'.

Unquenchable fire

This 'unquenchable fire' is mentioned in Luke 3:17 and we also find it in Mark 9:43. Others in the Bible do not use this extreme language, but John and Jesus do. The Greek word for 'unquenchable' is *asbestos* – the Greek word we have used to describe the hazardous, fire-resistant material. This is fire that cannot be stopped or satisfied. In other words, there is nothing partial or temporary about the judgement that Jesus brings: it is the final and complete judgement. With axe and winnow, Jesus is introduced as God who has come to clear out His world everyone and everything that is barren or fruitless or cut off from Him – and He has an unstoppable fire to burn it all up.

When the devil comes to try to stop Jesus in Matthew 4:1-11, it is the devil who has to retreat. Then Matthew quotes from Isaiah 9:1-2 telling us that the people in darkness, under the shadow of death, have seen the great light of Jesus shining on them. The Living God comes to drive out the devil, the darkness and death itself.

An oasis of Paradise

The eye witnesses of Jesus did not think of heaven and hell as ideas that belonged in some far off ethereal world, but as present realities, defined by the presence of Jesus Himself. Without Him there is exile, darkness and death under the slavery of the devil – but with His axe and winnow He brings divine fellowship, light and life.

To prove all this, Matthew 4 actually ends with Jesus specifically creating an island or an oasis of Paradise around Him as He drives out all the diseases, pains, demons and problems. It is as if Eden itself is happening in His very presence right there and then.

Elsewhere we see that even with a word or a touch Jesus can drive away disease or death. He can evict these intruders from His creation with total power and authority.

In Matthew 8:1-4 with a mere touch the leprosy disappears. In 8:14-15 a fever is driven out, followed by all kinds of diseases and demons in 8:16-17. Even when the weather is chaotic and unruly it can be brought back to order (8:23-27).

The demons living in the man at Gadara know that Jesus will one day not only drive them out but (according to verse 29) **torment** them. The man, reduced to living among the dead, controlled by violence and isolation, is set free. The demons prefer to be in the pigs, creatures that are symbolically cut off, outside the LORD's community and they rush down into those waters that had so recently risen up in chaotic defiance against Jesus.

All of this not only teaches us about what Jesus is doing right there and then, but also about His purpose for the whole creation.

The demons must be driven out and they know that this will happen 'at the appointed time'. Nature must be restored to its proper order. Human beings must be set free from demonic tyranny. Sickness and death must be cured once and for all. In Matthew 9:1-8 Jesus gets rid of both sin and paralysis, then the blind and mute are cured by His touch and in 9:25 death too is driven away by His hand.

To appreciate these actions as signs of who Jesus is and what He is ultimately doing we need to see them in the context of the parables.

Purging the world of all that is wrong

When we bought our house several years ago there were huge problems with it. The young lad we called in to look at the electrics emerged from the basement after an hour, ashen-faced and had to call his boss in for reinforcements!

When the workmen arrived with hammers and saws, and began to smash things and carry tons of rubbish and debris out to a truck it brought us great relief. They were coming to take away all that was wrong with the house and make it ready for renovation.

So too for those who hunger and thirst for God and His righteousness. The presence of Jesus with axe and winnow in hand brings great joy and relief. The workman has arrived! He has a cosmic rubbish truck with Him, a rubbish truck that can never be filled, ready to remove every last thing that is wrong with the world.

That is the big picture that we need in our minds as we listen to everything that Jesus teaches us about heaven and hell.

The Sermon on the Mount tells us that His kingdom brings comfort for our mourning and that we will inherit the whole earth in His righteousness and peace, when we see God ourselves… and yet, right now the wicked reject us, gnash their teeth against us, persecute us because their plans for the future are doomed to fail in the face of the divine Judge with His axe, winnow and fire.

Those that do not want Him or refuse to trust Him are good for nothing but to be 'thrown out and trampled underfoot' (Matt. 5:13). There is no place in Christ's good world for those who do not love and obey Him.

We tend to think that hell is only for the people that we think of as 'really evil, like Hitler', but our standards of judgement are deeply compromised and perverse. The axe and winnow of Jesus strike at targets that we are all too comfortable with. We might think hell is only for murderers and abusers, yet Jesus tells us His cleansing goes much deeper than that. The anger and common insults that are so frequent among us all will also be cut down and thrown into the fire (Matt. 5:21-22).

Gehenna – the place for the wicked

Now, stop for a moment and consider the word 'hell' that many of our English translations use in Matthew 5:21-22. The English word 'hell' is used to translate different Biblical words, and in the teaching of Jesus the word is used to describe both *Gehenna* and *Hades*.

The word in the Greek is the word *gehenna* and it is the word that Jesus generally uses when He is referring to the place where He will throw all the wicked at the end. So what is Gehenna?

Jesus mentions it several times:

> But I tell you that… anyone who says, 'You fool!' will be in danger of the fire of **Gehenna**. (Matt. 5:22)

If your right eye causes you to sin, gouge it out and throw it away. It is better for you to lose one part of your body than for your whole body to be thrown into **Gehenna**. (Matt. 5:29)

And if your right hand causes you to sin, cut it off and throw it away. It is better for you to lose one part of your body than for your whole body to go into **Gehenna**. (Matt. 5:30 and Mark 9:43-47)

Do not be afraid of those who kill the body but cannot kill the soul. Rather, be afraid of the One who can destroy both soul and body in **Gehenna**. (Matt. 10:28 and Luke 12:5)

And if your eye causes you to sin, gouge it out and throw it away. It is better for you to enter life with one eye than to have two eyes and be thrown into the fire of **Gehenna**. (Matt. 18:9)

Woe to you, teachers of the law and Pharisees, you hypocrites! You travel over land and sea to win a single convert, and when he becomes one, you make him twice as much a son of **Gehenna** as you are. (Matt. 23:15)

You snakes! You brood of vipers! How will you escape being condemned to **Gehenna**? (Matt. 23:33)

Jesus' brother, James, is the only other person to use this word in James 3:6:

The tongue also is a fire, a world of evil among the parts of the body. It corrupts the whole person, sets the whole course of his life on fire, and is itself set on fire by **Gehenna**.

A common myth

What is this place called Gehenna? The problem is that there are all kinds of myths and rumours about it, conjured up from outside the Bible. I have to confess that I've fallen for one of the common ones over the years. A popular myth says that Gehenna was a rubbish tip outside of Jerusalem at the time of Jesus. People have claimed all kinds of things about this place. Some say that there were fires always burning at the rubbish tip as the waste from the city was burned up. I have even heard somebody claim that there were stray dogs at this dump fighting over scraps of meat that people had thrown away and people could hear the dogs gnashing their teeth on the bones. All this is supposed to be in the background when Jesus speaks about Gehenna.

However, nothing of this is ever mentioned in the Bible! The Bible never speaks of a rubbish tip near Jerusalem called Gehenna. There is not one single reference to this rubbish tip in any other literature from the time – whether Josephus, Philo, the Dead Sea Scrolls or rabbinical teaching. And there is no archaeological support for this common myth whatsoever.

So where did the idea come from? I'm told that the first reference to Gehenna as a rubbish tip outside Jerusalem came from a rabbinical teacher called Kimhi in the early 13th century A.D. In other words, nobody knew anything of this idea for 1,200 years until someone dreamed it up.[1]

---

1. 'The traditional explanation for this seems to go back to Rabbi David Kimhi's commentary on Psalm 27 (around 1200 c.e.). He remarked the following concerning the valley beneath Jerusalem's walls: "Gehenna is a repugnant place, into which filth and cadavers are thrown, and in which

The Valley of Hinnom

We need to stay within the text of the Bible to understand what Jesus is talking about. The word *Gehenna* simply means the valley of Hinnom (*gê-hinnōm* – Joshua 18:16 in the Septuagint refers to Gaienna). The Bible tells us about this Valley because it was the place that Baal and the Canaanite gods were worshipped through child sacrifice. It was the place of most hostility and opposition to the ways of the LORD God. It was everything He hated:

> (Josiah) desecrated Topheth, which was in the Valley of Ben Hinnom, so no one could use it to sacrifice his son or daughter in the fire to Molech. (2 Kings 23:10)

> Ahaz was twenty years old when he became king, and he reigned in Jerusalem sixteen years. Unlike David his father, he did not do what was right in the eyes of the LORD. He walked in the ways of the kings of Israel and also made cast idols for worshiping the Baals. He burned sacrifices in the Valley of Ben Hinnom and sacrificed his sons in the fire, following the detestable ways of the nations the LORD had driven out before the Israelites. (2 Chron. 28:1-3)

> (Manasseh) sacrificed his sons in the fire in the Valley of Ben Hinnom, practiced sorcery, divination and witchcraft, and

---

fires perpetually burn in order to consume the filth and bones; on which account, by analogy, the judgement of the wicked is called 'Gehenna'." Kimhi's otherwise plausible suggestion, however, finds no support in literary sources or archaeological data from the intertestamental or rabbinic periods. There is no evidence that the valley was, in fact, a garbage dump, and thus his explanation is insufficient' ('Gehenna: The Topography of Hell', *Biblical Archaeologist* 49/3 [1986], 188-89).

consulted mediums and spiritists. He did much evil in the eyes of the LORD, provoking him to anger. (2 Chron. 33:6)

This next reference from Jeremiah links into several of the things that are said about the fate of the wicked, not only in Jesus' own teaching but also in the book of Revelation:

> 'The people of Judah have done evil in my eyes', declares the LORD. 'They have set up their detestable idols in the house that bears my Name and have defiled it. They have built the high places of Topheth in the Valley of Ben Hinnom to burn their sons and daughters in the fire – something I did not command, nor did it enter my mind. So beware, the days are coming', declares the LORD, 'when people will no longer call it Topheth or the Valley of Ben Hinnom, but the Valley of Slaughter, for they will bury the dead in Topheth until there is no more room. Then the carcasses of this people will become food for the birds of the air and the beasts of the earth, and there will be no one to frighten them away.' (Jer. 7:30-33)

To be thrown into that valley means being located with Baal and Molech; with child sacrifice and sexual immorality; with everything that God hates. The Valley of Hinnom was the place of total rejection of the LORD God. He would make it the place where His enemies would be destroyed.

When Jesus speaks of Gehenna, then, He has something more sinister in mind than a civic rubbish tip!

To be thrown into Gehenna, in the language of Jesus, means that a person's life is as offensive to Him as all those things that were done in the Valley of Hinnom. He looks at a person as belonging to **that** rebellion against Him.

If a person has lived against Christ then they will finally be put in the place where they really belong – a place that reveals both their opposition to Him and their destruction with all that defiles His world.

Gehenna, then, is not only a place of opposition against God, a place of spiritual darkness, rebellion, cruelty and sin, but it is also a place of burning. Just as Sodom and Gomorrah stand as examples of not only evil behaviour but also destructive fire from the LORD, so Gehenna is Christ's way of referring to both the place of rebellion and the fire of its destruction.

The only possible future in this world is with Jesus, in the Spirit, seeing the Father's face. Only those in Christ's kingdom will see the Father's face and inherit the earth. Everybody else will be taken away, thrown out, cast into the fire, left outside when the door is slammed shut.

The clock is ticking

All these shocking ways of speaking of that final and absolute conclusion to the day of judgement come from the teaching of Jesus. The clock is ticking: the hour of the end has been set by the Father. Even Jesus the Eternal Son does not know when that hour will come. There is limited time and limited opportunity to make peace with the Living God in Christ before that final hour arrives. It is better to sacrifice anything and everything to be part of Christ's kingdom, to be part of that everlasting future with God. If we are not known to Jesus then our home is the fire of Gehenna.

A time of reckoning is coming and it is much better to settle the matter now (Matt. 5:25-26). In fact, any loss right now is good value if we can enter the kingdom, even the loss of our most precious parts (5:27-30). The Father rewards those who are concerned only for His attention. Those who live for praise right now receive just that (6:1-18).

It is investments in heaven that matter – looking upward and forward to that coming kingdom of the future – 6:19-24.

Looking up

It is the upwards and forwards perspective that saturates the teaching of Jesus. When He prays He looks up to heaven, because His heart, mind, soul and strength are focused on the Father in heaven, on Zion, on the City of God – on the coming kingdom. Everything is done with concern only for the attention and praise of the Father in heaven.

Jesus Himself is not from below but from above – John 8:23. His kingdom is not from this world, but the kingdom of heaven.

When Jesus exposes the danger of riches in Luke 16 He shows us how the poor man, Lazarus, is carried by the angels to Paradise, to be in the company of Abraham when he dies. In this passing age Lazarus may have had no comfort and been overlooked by everybody, but looking only to his heavenly Father he was received into a glorious inheritance:

> The time came when the beggar died and the angels carried him to Abraham's side. The rich man also died and was buried. In Hades, where he was in torment, he looked up and saw Abraham far away, with Lazarus by his side. (Luke 16:22-23)

The fact that both Elijah and Moses meet with Jesus on the mountain in Luke 9:28-36 reveals the vitality of those who have gone into heaven. It is perhaps easier to imagine how Elijah might still be alive in a miraculous sense because he was taken bodily up to heaven, yet Moses' body was buried by the LORD. Nevertheless, the disciples knew who these two ancient saints were and they were clearly so alive that they could speak to Jesus about His coming sacrificial work on the cross.

If we die without Jesus we sink down into the frustrated bitterness of the 'kingdom of the dead', as we might call Hades. If we die with Jesus then He gathers us into that heavenly kingdom where there is fellowship, rest and a joyful waiting for the renewal of all things.

The same principle comes out with the thief on the cross who asks Jesus to remember him.

In other words, when we are known by Jesus we pass over from the control of death into the power of life, the gushing spring of life that flows from Jesus. He is the Spirit-filled Man – the One who has life without limit.

If Jesus knows us then we never die, but still live even when our body dies.

> Very truly I tell you, whoever obeys my word **will never see death.** (John 8:52)

> whoever lives by believing in me **will never die**. (John 11:26)

Think of the situation of that thief dying next to Jesus. There is no possibility for him to do anything good with his life. He can do no religious rituals and he is utterly cursed according to Deuteronomy 21:22-23. He cannot offer what the law requires and he is utterly immobile, nailed to that wooden cross. What possible hope can there be for him?

He is dying next to the Immortal God, the Lord Jesus Christ. He does nothing more than call out to Jesus. What can Jesus do to help him? Jesus is just as immobile and powerless as he is. Yet, Jesus is the King of the eternal Kingdom of Heaven and was actually working an omnipotent work in His very weakness and death. The thief could look to Jesus and find the impossible assurance that even then, in that death-soaked place, he could find a life that was stronger than death in Jesus:

> He said, 'Jesus, remember me when you come into your kingdom.' Jesus answered him, 'Truly I tell you, today you will be with me in paradise.' (Luke 23:42-43)

We will look at being absent from the body but present with Jesus in paradise in more detail in the next chapter, but for now we must note how wonderful it must have been to go from the horror of that cursed death to the wonderful blessings of the third heaven with Jesus, all in one day!

To be remembered by Jesus is in the end the only thing that matters.

If He knows us on that final day then we will be carried on into His new creation future, His marriage feast. Yet, even now, before that final day, the thief was promised by Jesus, 'today you will be with me in paradise'. Every day Jesus directs us to focus our attention on our Father who is in heaven.

In this passing age, we look up, but only because we are ultimately looking forward.

The true day of judgement and resurrection

Jesus Christ looked **up** to heaven, but He lived with a constant **forward** focus, looking ahead to that day of judgement.

We could spend a whole book on the subject of heaven and hell in relation to the cross and resurrection of Jesus, but we must make a few comments now.

The death of Jesus is nothing less than the true day of judgement occurring in the middle of history. In John 19:13-14 Pilate places his judgement seat on the temple pavement at the time of the passover preparation. As in heaven there is the pavement under the feet of the LORD God, so this is reflected on earth as judgement is passed against Jesus.

In Matthew 27:50-53, when Jesus dies, it is as if the events of the final day of God happen right there and then around the crucified God.

> When Jesus had cried out again in a loud voice, he gave up his spirit. At that moment the curtain of the temple was torn in two from top to bottom. The earth shook and the rocks split. The tombs broke open and the bodies of many holy people who had died were raised to life. They came out of the tombs, and after Jesus' resurrection they went into the holy city and appeared to many people. (Matt. 27:50-53)

The earthquake, the resurrection, the removal of the barrier between heaven and earth – all this finds its centre at the true moment of new creation, the resurrection of Jesus Himself:

192

> After the Sabbath, at dawn on the first day of the week, Mary Magdalene and the other Mary went to look at the tomb. There was a violent earthquake, for an angel of the Lord came down from heaven and, going to the tomb, rolled back the stone and sat on it. His appearance was like lightning, and his clothes were white as snow. The guards were so afraid of him that they shook and became like dead men. (Matt. 28:1-4)

The old order of the world seems so flat and two-dimensional compared to the integrated, spiritual-physical brightness of the resurrection world.

The risen Jesus is the same as before... and yet also different. He cooks breakfast for His friends (John 21:9-12). He walks with His people, explaining the Scriptures to them. He retains His wounds, as trophies of His victory, and yet at the same time there is something about Him and the way He moves about that shows He is part of a new order.

Jesus was always looking ahead to His death and resurrection; to the transformation of all things that He would bring about. However, even as He looks to that cosmic redemption, He constantly speaks warnings about that day.

Constant warnings

Time after time, Jesus tells stories that make us face up to that day when the Son of Man comes in all His glory; when the wedding feast begins; when the master returns to His household; when the bridegroom arrives; when the harvest is gathered in and the weeds are thrown away into the fire.

In Matthew 6:30 the grass is here today and tomorrow thrown into the fire. The default path right now leads to destruction in the future. Right now it may seem easy and everybody goes along this road: the great and the good, the clever and the religious. Yet what is the future destination? Destruction.

Recently a view of God has arisen that imagines that in the end most if not all people will finally be accepted and forgiven regardless of the road they have walked, whatever their basic religious commitment, regardless of their trust in Jesus. But Jesus repeatedly states in the clearest possible terms that most people will end up in destruction. Only a few will go through the narrow gate and walk the narrow way of life:

> Enter through the narrow gate. For wide is the gate and broad is the road that leads to destruction, and **many enter through it**. But small is the gate and narrow the road that leads to life, and **only a few find it**. (Matt. 7:13-14)

The identity of those on the road to life is not a mystery. Jesus says that it is quite obvious – those that love Him, obey Him and bear the fruit of His life and kingdom. There are many people who speak a lot about Him, do all the religious stuff, even do extraordinary things, yet they do not love and trust Jesus Himself.

In fact, Jesus states that the future day of judgement will be a harvest, when the wheat and fruitful plants are gathered into the barn but the weeds and barren branches and fruitless trees are cut down and thrown into the fire. The false teachers who bear no fruit will be thrown into the fire – Matthew 7:19. So, even now as we see fruit growing in the lives of the followers of Jesus we can see something of what will be revealed on the day of harvesting and burning.

Weeding, sorting, burning

The parable of the wheat and the weeds is right at the heart of all Jesus' teaching:

Jesus told them another parable: 'The kingdom of heaven is like a man who sowed good seed in his field. But while everyone was sleeping, his enemy came and sowed weeds among the wheat, and went away. When the wheat sprouted and formed heads, then the weeds also appeared. The owner's servants came to him and said, "Sir, didn't you sow good seed in your field? Where then did the weeds come from?" "An enemy did this," he replied. The servants asked him, "Do you want us to go and pull them up?" "No," he answered, "because while you are pulling the weeds, you may root up the wheat with them. Let both grow together until the harvest. At that time I will tell the harvesters: First collect the weeds and tie them in bundles to be burned; then gather the wheat and bring it into my barn."'… Then he left the crowd and went into the house. His disciples came to him and said, 'Explain to us the parable of the weeds in the field.' He answered, 'The one who sowed the good seed is the Son of Man. The field is the world, and the good seed stands for the sons of the kingdom. The weeds are the sons of the evil one, and the enemy who sows them is the devil. The harvest is the end of the age, and the harvesters are angels. As the weeds are pulled up and burned in the fire, so it will be at the end of the age. The Son of Man will send out his angels, and **they will weed out of his kingdom everything that causes sin and all who do evil**. They will throw them into the fiery furnace, where there will be weeping and gnashing of teeth. Then the righteous will shine like the sun in the kingdom of their Father. He who has ears, let him hear.' (Matt. 13:24-43)

Right **now** in this passing age there is confusion, but **then** there will be perfect clarity. All will be revealed for what it really is. The Son of Man is coming with the angelic armies of heaven to 'weed out' of His kingdom everything that causes sin and all who do evil.

The day of judgement is sometimes portrayed as a cosmic, secret lottery where we all find out whether we picked a winning ticket or not. This could not be further from the way that Jesus speaks. There is nothing arbitrary or secret or random about the Day of harvest; the Day of revelation; the Day of sorting and burning; the Day when the door will be eternally closed on the chaos and darkness.

The world belongs to the Father and the Son in the power of the Spirit. It is the territory of the kingdom of God, the kingdom of heaven. Right now the earth is in rebellion with servants who are not doing their master's will. It is like a farmer's field or a vineyard, filled with plants that produce no useful crop, badly managed by selfish tenants, over-run by weeds. The owner is coming to sort out the mess. He will arrest and execute the bad tenants. He will clear out all the weeds and throw them on the fire. He will carefully tend the plants and cut down all those that have no fruit for him.

He will be left with a clean and clear field, ready to be personally managed by himself, ready to produce a glorious and everlasting crop of fruit without any weeds or enemies or opposition ever again.

That is essentially the consistent teaching of Jesus through all His life. The imagery can vary. It might be like a large net dragged into a fishing boat:

> ... the kingdom of heaven is like a net that was let down into the lake and caught all kinds of fish. When it was full, the fishermen pulled it up on the shore. Then they sat down and collected the good fish in baskets, but threw the bad away. This is how it will be at the end of the age. The angels will come and separate the wicked from the righteous and throw them into the fiery furnace, where there will be weeping and gnashing of teeth. (Matt. 13:47-50)

But note the consistent features: the harvest; the sorting; the burning of what is worth nothing to the owner or the fisherman or the farmer or the king.

Perhaps the most striking fact about Jesus' teaching on the day of judgement is that He essentially speaks about it from the perspective of the farmer, fisherman or king rather than from the perspective of the plants, tenants, fish or servants. The judgement is ultimately about what is useful or valuable to **Him**. Anything that has no use to Him is simply thrown into the fire.

Am I useful or fruitful?

Jesus puts this in different ways.

To be useful or fruitful can also be stated as simply as whether Jesus knows us or not on that day of judgement.

If we are known to Jesus because we have trusted Him and followed Him, then we will have fruit for Him, fruit that comes not from the fact that we have worked hard to produce it but fruit that comes simply from the fact that we are *connected to Jesus Himself*.

In the end He is the only fruitful one. He is the plant that produces fruit for eternity and we can only ever be fruitful branches attached to Him. If we are not connected to Him, then He does not know us and we cannot produce any fruit. On that day of judgement we will be barren and unknown, fit only for the fire:

> I am the true vine, and my Father is the gardener. He cuts off every branch in me that bears no fruit, while every branch that does bear fruit he prunes so that it will be even more fruitful. You are already clean because of the word I have spoken to you. Remain in me, and I will remain in you. No branch can bear fruit by itself; it must remain in the vine. Neither can you bear fruit unless you remain in me. I am the vine; you are the branches. If a man remains in me and I in him, he will bear much fruit; apart from me you can do nothing. If anyone does not remain in me, he is like a branch that is thrown away and withers; such branches are picked up, thrown into the fire and burned. If you remain in me and my words remain in you, ask whatever you wish, and it will be given you. This is to my Father's glory, that you bear much fruit, showing yourselves to be my disciples. (John 15:1-8)

I never knew you…

The final and ultimate judgement is that He never knew us. What makes that final judgement so bad is not simply being cast into the fire, but being shut out from the presence of Jesus Himself. Matthew 7:23 states it in terrifying terms –

'Then I will tell them plainly, "I never knew you. Away from **me**, you evildoers!".'

In Matthew 25 in Jesus' vivid description of the day of sorting when the goats are revealed as those who have not produced the fruit of remaining in Jesus, Jesus speaks the most terrible words of judgement – (v. 41) 'Depart from **me**, you who are cursed, into the eternal fire prepared for the devil and his angels.'

Jesus is Himself the life and light of the world. He is our justice and peace, our joy and delight. He is the source of the creative diversity and wonder of the whole creation. He is the logic and purpose of the heavens and the earth.

To be eternally cut off from Him, cursed, to be shut out with the devil and everything else that is opposed to Jesus means that in that place of outer darkness, that Valley of Hinnom where all that He hates festers away, there could never be any hope or life or order or peace or purpose or forgiveness.

Weeping and gnashing of teeth

Jesus constantly describes this fate as a place of weeping and gnashing of teeth. On seven occasions He refers to people gnashing their teeth when they are thrown out on the day of judgement (Matt. 8:12; 13:42,50; 22:13; 24:51; 25:30 and Luke 13:28).

Sometimes people imagine that the gnashing of teeth comes from people being in agony, but that is not what the phrase means in the Bible.

In Acts 7:54 when Stephen gets to the conclusion of his sermon to the temple leaders, accusing them of betraying and murdering the Righteous One, their reaction is striking:

'When they heard this, they were furious and **gnashed their teeth at him**.' And in verses 57-58, 'yelling at the top of their voices, they all rushed at him, dragged him out of the city and began to stone him.'

The gnashing of teeth is all about anger and opposition. Psalm 35 and 37 put it so clearly. When the wicked see the righteous inheriting the earth and all the blessing that the LORD has for them they will gnash their teeth at the LORD and His people:

> … when I stumbled, they gathered in glee; attackers gathered against me when I was unaware. They slandered me without ceasing. Like the ungodly they maliciously mocked; **they gnashed their teeth at me**. O Lord, how long will you look on? Rescue my life from their ravages, my precious life from these lions. I will give you thanks in the great assembly; among throngs of people I will praise you. Let not those gloat over me who are my enemies… (Ps. 35:15-19)

> …evil men will be cut off, but those who hope in the LORD will inherit the land. A little while, and the wicked will be no more; though you look for them, they will not be found. But the meek will inherit the land and enjoy great peace. The wicked plot against the righteous and **gnash their teeth at them**; but the Lord laughs at the wicked, for he knows their day is coming. The wicked draw the sword and bend the bow to bring down the poor and needy, to slay those whose ways are upright. (Ps. 37:9-14)

The wicked gnash their teeth against the righteous even now in this age, but even more so in the age to come.

On that day when all is revealed, when the truth is made clear, when the true nature of each person is exposed, then everything comes into the open. There will be no veneer of civilisation and respectability covering over and containing the true desires and hatred of the human heart then. The selfishness and evil desires that enslave will be let loose so that all are seen for what they are.

The desire to ignore, reject and replace God will no longer be hidden under the business of day to day life. On that final day the world will gnash its teeth against the Lord Jesus and His bride, and what a cause of celebration and relief it will be when that gnashing, snarling beast is thrown into the eternal 'cage' in the outer darkness, the unquenchable fire, never to be remembered ever again.

The renewal of all things

As we conclude we should remember that though the return of Jesus is a day of harvesting, revealing, sorting, burning and shutting out, yet all of that is only a **preparation** for the real future – the renewal of all things, as Jesus describes it in Matthew 19:28.

Nobody else in the Bible has such a comprehensive and profound description of the future. The apostles will later try to open up what Jesus meant by this, but nothing else in the Bible quite packs so much into so little.

The heavens and the earth, the animals and the plants, the kingdoms of this world and all human society, the sun, moon and stars, our very bodies – all will be renewed. And yet even that is only part of the preparation.

The real goal of it all is the wedding feast and the marriage of Christ and the Church that stretches away into all eternity.

> I say to you that many will come from the east and the west, and will take their places at the feast with Abraham, Isaac and Jacob in the kingdom of heaven. (Matt. 8:11)

> The kingdom of heaven is like a king who prepared a wedding banquet for his son. (Matt. 22:2)

> At that time the kingdom of heaven will be like ten virgins who took their lamps and went out to meet the bridegroom. (Matt. 25:1)

The marriage of Christ and the Church was always the real meaning and purpose of the universe. All that came before was simply preparation.

The reason the wicked with their fruitless lives and gnashing teeth have to be taken away is so that the creation can become the everlasting family home of righteousness, when the Father will come down to dwell with His eternal Son and His redeemed Bride in the fellowship of the Spirit forever more.

> *Lo! He comes with clouds descending,*
> *Once for favoured sinners slain;*
> *Thousand thousand saints attending,*
> *Swell the triumph of His train:*
> *Hallelujah! Hallelujah! Hallelujah!*
> *God appears on earth to reign.*

Every eye shall now behold Him
Robed in dreadful majesty;
Those who set at naught and sold Him,
Pierced and nailed Him to the tree,
Deeply wailing, deeply wailing, deeply wailing,
Shall the true Messiah see.

Yea, Amen! let all adore Thee,
High on Thine eternal throne;
Saviour, take the power and glory,
Claim the kingdom for Thine own;
O come quickly! O come quickly! O come quickly!
Everlasting God, come down!

CHAPTER 9

THE CHURCH – HEAVEN RIGHT NOW

A CHURCH can be a genuine experience of heaven.

When the local church is putting on the new humanity of Jesus, saying 'no!' to old, selfish desires and saying 'yes!' to self-sacrifice and serving others, it gives a real glimpse of the kind of life that will go on forever in the renewed creation.

When Jesus is at the centre of our church, leading us to the Father in praise, prayer and service, we experience what life is really all about, what we were created for. When we share what we have, love one another with sincerity, speak the truth together, walk in step with the Spirit, enjoying the friendship of Jesus and the love of the Father, then we can really taste what eternal life is all about.

However, when false teachers come in and spread division, when the love of money controls the leaders, when immorality rots away behind the respectable surface, when divisions and factions form, when we take pride in ourselves, when we bring 'religion' into the church, then the church is an experience of the godless life of hell itself. When the church becomes like the world then the chaos and frustration of hell appear.

The local church is a lens through which we see life and death, heaven and hell, Christ and the devil. The letters of the New Testament are written with such passion and intensity because the stakes are so high; the issues are so weighty. If false teaching is not rooted out and replaced with the living word of Christ Himself then the Church will show off the reality of hell rather than heaven – eternal destruction rather than eternal life. If dark desires and deceptive doctrine are allowed to run riot then there will be nothing but darkness and chaos.

When people have experienced hell in godless 'churches' we can understand why they are so repelled by the very idea of 'church' for the rest of their lives.

Eternal life – the life of love in the church right now

In Ephesians chapter 4 and 5 Paul sets out the contrast between the futile thinking of the pagan world and the truth in Jesus. His great argument is that the local church draws her life from Christ and is equipped by the Spirit to live the life of God Himself. Eternal life, the very life of God Himself, is not some secret or abstract idea. Eternal life – the life of the ages that flows out of the Father, through the Son and in the Spirit – is that life of love that the local church is designed to live now and forever.

By contrast, a life cut off from Jesus is revealed in selfishness and sin; despair and depression; emptiness and frustration; division and anger.

Paul shows how Christ has provided everything necessary for the local church in the Spirit, whether gifts and leadership or that eternal life that flows from Him through the local fellowship. Yet, this wonderful experience of the life of heaven may all be turned around and ruined if we allow the futile thinking of the pagan world to control our minds. Once we teach ourselves those false doctrines of darkness, selfishness and doubt, so everything in life begins to unravel and we fall into frustration, insensitivity and a feeling that God is far away or not there at all!

> So I tell you this, and insist on it in the Lord, that you must no longer live as the Gentiles do, in the futility of their thinking. They are darkened in their understanding and separated from the life of God because of the ignorance that is in them due to the hardening of their hearts. Having lost all sensitivity, they have given themselves over to sensuality so as to indulge in every kind of impurity, with a continual lust for more. You, however, did not come to know Christ that way. Surely you heard of him and were taught in him in accordance with the truth that is in Jesus. You were taught, with regard to your former way of life, to put off your old self, which is being corrupted by its deceitful desires; to be made new in the attitude of your minds; and to put on the new self, created to be like God in true righteousness and holiness. (Eph. 4:17-24)

- The futile way of the Gentiles is hell.
- The truth that is in Jesus is heaven.

Note the features of the way of the unbelieving world: futile thinking; darkened understanding; separated from the life of God; hardened hearts; loss of sensitivity; given over to sensuality; indulging in impurity; a continual lust for more – with the frustration of no satisfaction. This vivid and accurate description of the broad way of destruction gives a real sense of how hell will be – a place of gnawing frustration, uncontrolled desires, lack of honest feeling and, most of all, alienation from the Father, Son and Spirit.

When the Church turns away from the way, the truth and the life of Jesus this experience of hell comes upon us. In fact, because of the close bonds of the local church and the fact that it is the very battleground of the universe, there can be a special intensity to these symptoms of divine alienation.

The Spirit or the devil

Paul literally associates the devil with the futile way of ignorance and the Holy Spirit of God with the redeemed life of love:

> Therefore each of you must put off falsehood and speak truthfully to his neighbour, for we are all members of one body. 'In your anger do not sin': Do not let the sun go down while you are still angry, and do not give the devil a foothold. He who has been stealing must steal no longer, but must work, doing something useful with his own hands, that he may have something to share with those in need. Do not let any unwholesome talk come out of your mouths, but only what is helpful for building others up according to their needs, that it may benefit those who listen. And do not grieve the Holy Spirit of God, with whom you were sealed for the day of redemption. Get rid of all bitterness, rage and anger, brawling and slander, along with every form of

malice. Be kind and compassionate to one another, forgiving each other, just as in Christ God forgave you. Be imitators of God, therefore, as dearly loved children and live a life of love, just as Christ loved us and gave himself up for us as a fragrant offering and sacrifice to God. (Eph. 4:25–5:2)

We can see why the Holy Spirit would be grieved when His native life of God and the fellowship of heaven is dragged into the polluted and decaying death of the devil with his lies, anger and laziness.

Throughout the letters we find this constant contrast between the pattern of life and the pattern of death, the way that leads to heaven and the way that leads to hell.

The kingdom of God – the eternal life of God

The Kingdom of God is the Kingdom that will never pass away, the Kingdom whose citizens will rule over the whole creation with the King forever and ever. All the kingdoms of this world will finally be swallowed up by the Kingdom of our God. So being genuine, true citizens of the Kingdom of heaven is the critical issue in terms of our eternal life and destiny.

It has often been noted how the teaching of Jesus Himself focused on the Kingdom of God or the Kingdom of heaven. As the King of the Kingdom He is focused on the Kingdom, but as citizens of His Kingdom we, along with the prophets and apostles, tend to focus on the King Himself.

That same theme runs all the way through the letters as well, even though the words 'Kingdom of God' do not occur so often. The Kingdom of God is the eternal life of God, the Spirit's rule of goodness, righteousness and purity:

> For the kingdom of God is not a matter of eating and drinking, but of righteousness, peace and joy in the Holy Spirit, because anyone who serves Christ in this way is pleasing to God and approved by men. (Rom. 14:17-18)

That same contrast between the experience of heaven (the Kingdom of God) and the experience of hell (the way of the flesh) comes out time and again throughout Paul's letters. Though we all once lived as citizens of hell, through the death and resurrection of Jesus, by the power of the Spirit, we have become citizens of the Kingdom of God:

> Do you not know that the wicked will not inherit the kingdom of God? Do not be deceived: Neither the sexually immoral nor idolaters nor adulterers nor male prostitutes nor homosexual offenders nor thieves nor the greedy nor drunkards nor slanderers nor swindlers will inherit the kingdom of God. And that is what some of you were. But you were washed, you were sanctified, you were justified in the name of the Lord Jesus Christ and by the Spirit of our God. (1 Cor. 6:9-11)

This is here and now!

Sometimes people become concerned about the reality of heaven and hell. Are there really such ultimate and eternal destinies for good and evil? Is it just wishful thinking to imagine that evil will finally be eternally judged, thrown out and punished? Is it simply too good to be true that the life of the church will carry on beyond death in heaven and then on into a glorious new creation future?

My own son Jonathan, when he was quite young, had some very disturbed nights after his teacher at school explained how one ancient civilisation believed that after death there was nothing but darkness and non-existence. The knowledge that people thought such things was too much for his young mind!

Heaven and hell do exist. However, far from belonging **only** to some future time or an invisible realm, they are manifest right here and now among us.

The community of heaven, the fellowship of the new creation, eternal life itself can be clearly seen as the Church lives by the Spirit, rejecting the decaying life of the flesh. In the same way, the isolation of hell, the frustration and depression of the outer darkness, the broad way of destruction can be clearly seen when we follow the selfish desires of the flesh in cowardice, pride, hatred and division:

> So I say, live by the Spirit, and you will not gratify the desires of the sinful nature. For the sinful nature desires what is contrary to the Spirit, and the Spirit what is contrary to the sinful nature. They are in conflict with each other, so that you do not do what you want. But if you are led by the Spirit, you are not under law. The acts of the sinful nature are obvious: sexual immorality, impurity and debauchery; idolatry and witchcraft; hatred, discord, jealousy, fits of rage, selfish ambition, dissensions, factions and envy; drunkenness, orgies, and the like. I warn you, as I did before, that those who live like this will not inherit the kingdom of God. (Gal. 5:16-21)

Visible signs – right now!

I watched a TV programme recently. A man had an appointment with a personal trainer for advice on health and fitness.

211

The man was a smoker, ate huge amounts of fried food and drank several cans of beer every evening. As he struggled to climb even the stairs to the fitness studio, gasping for breath with sweat pouring from him, the trainer remarked, 'It's not just that he is bringing about his early death – this lifestyle is already like death.'

In the same way, a life of selfishness, doubt, greed, anger, lusts and pride is just as obviously racing to damnation. There is no place for any of those ways in the eternal life of the new creation.

Those ways already stink of death and hell.

Of course the anger of God will be expressed against all such sinful pollution but the outcome of such a life is already obvious long before the day of final justice.

I watched another TV programme (I honestly don't spend my life watching these!) investigating the harmful effects of junk food. We were introduced to a man in his late 50s who had eaten only fresh fruit and vegetables, with regular aerobic exercise, since he was young. It was incredible. He looked as if he was about 22! Not matter how cynical I get about fitness fads, when I remember this man I have to admit there is something to be said for healthy living. The consequences of how we treat our physical bodies tell us truths about the way we treat our souls, our very life itself.

It is not just that the final outcome of a life of healthy living is 'life' – but all the way through that life, there is energy and vitality. In that same way, as we follow the Lord of life in the way of life, so the signs of life – eternal life – are seen and experienced beginning right now and going on into that eternal future. The signs of real, eternal life can be bursting out even when our physical body is weak and dying. Our physical body will die no matter how carefully we live, but if we come to the Lord of life then we can enter into life every day and become more full of true life even as our body is wasting away:

> When you were slaves to sin, you were free from the control of righteousness. What benefit did you reap at that time from the things you are now ashamed of? Those things result in death! But now that you have been set free from sin and have become slaves to God, the benefit you reap leads to holiness, and the result is eternal life. For the wages of sin is death, but the gift of God is eternal life in Christ Jesus our Lord. (Rom. 6:20-23)

If we are enslaved to the evil and selfish desires of death then we are already falling into the eternal death of hell. If we are freed from that decay and instead the fruitfulness of the Spirit is growing up in our daily lives then we are already enjoying that overflowing eternal life that will go on forever in the fellowship of the Father, Son and Holy Spirit.

It is not that we enter into a sinless perfection when we trust Jesus, but that the whole direction of our lives changes. We can never be at peace with sin and selfishness ever again once we cross over from death to life. Every day we need to come to ask for forgiveness, for cleansing, because we can no longer tolerate the clinging shame and filth of sin upon us. The perfect, sinless life of Jesus is our true life and we always look to Him for our righteousness:

> Since, then, you have been raised with Christ, set your hearts on things above, where Christ is seated at the right

hand of God. Set your minds on things above, not on earthly things. For you died, and your life is now hidden with Christ in God. When Christ, who is your life, appears, then you also will appear with him in glory. Put to death, therefore, whatever belongs to your earthly nature: sexual immorality, impurity, lust, evil desires and greed, which is idolatry. Because of these, the wrath of God is coming. You used to walk in these ways, in the life you once lived. But now you must rid yourselves of all such things as these: anger, rage, malice, slander, and filthy language from your lips. Do not lie to each other, since you have taken off your old self with its practices and have put on the new self, which is being renewed in knowledge in the image of its Creator. Here there is no Greek or Jew, circumcised or uncircumcised, barbarian, Scythian, slave or free, but Christ is all, and is in all. (Col. 3:1-11)

For the grace of God that brings salvation has appeared to all men. It teaches us to say 'No' to ungodliness and worldly passions, and to live self-controlled, upright and godly lives in this present age, while we wait for the blessed hope – the glorious appearing of our great God and Saviour, Jesus Christ, who gave himself for us to redeem us from all wickedness and to purify for himself a people that are his very own, eager to do what is good. (Titus 2:11-14)

He gives us what we want

This basic understanding of reality is so important because it explains why the great future hope of the Bible is totally consistent with and the natural conclusion to the basic patterns of day to day life in the church.

Right now we see eternal life and eternal destruction being expressed all around us. When Jesus Christ comes to make the final division between light and darkness He will reveal what has already been true throughout our lives: His final judgement delivers the way of death to its final deathly destination and His way of life will also be given its final destination of an entire universe filled with nothing but light and life.

Hell – left in our sin forever

In Romans 1 God's response to our wilful ignorance of Christ is to allow us to fall into those evil desires that we love more than Him. The most terrible judgement of all is for Him to give us what we want, if our hearts are captured by the way that leads to unending death. The worst fate of all is to be enslaved by an evil love; to love what corrupts and destroys us.

The judgement of sin **is** sin.

In one sense the Bible describes hell as the punishment for sin, but in another sense hell is the logical outcome of sin. The worst punishment that we can ever receive for our sin is to be given over to it and left to wallow in it forever.

We think that we want selfish pleasures and the flesh, yet to be given over to the power of the flesh is to be trapped in a decaying and dying cycle of corruption and frustration.

We so often experience this in our sexuality because this lies so deep at the centre of who we are as the glorious image-bearers of God. When a man and a woman are united together as one flesh they can experience the unity of the Trinity in an incredible way. We can experience something of that passionate love between Christ and the church. In all of life we can have an appropriate level of love and fellowship, distinctly shaped by our gender as men and women. Our desire for intimacy with each other is the powerful drive that defines our true humanity. The flesh twists all this into a selfish and demanding drive: lust rather than love; demand rather than service; taking rather than giving:

> God gave them over in the sinful desires of their hearts to sexual impurity for the degrading of their bodies with one another. They exchanged the truth of God for a lie, and worshiped and served created things rather than the Creator – who is forever praised. Amen. Because of this, God gave them over to shameful lusts. Even their women exchanged natural relations for unnatural ones. In the same way the men also abandoned natural relations with women and were inflamed with lust for one another. Men committed indecent acts with other men, and received in themselves the due penalty for their perversion. Furthermore, since they did not think it worthwhile to retain the knowledge of God, he gave them over to a depraved mind, to do what ought not to be done. They have become filled with every kind of wickedness, evil, greed and depravity. They are full of envy, murder, strife, deceit and malice. They are gossips, slanderers, God-haters, insolent, arrogant and boastful; they invent ways of doing evil; they disobey their parents; they are senseless, faithless, heartless, ruthless. Although they know God's righteous decree that those who do such things deserve death, they not only continue to do these very things but also approve of those who practise them. (Rom. 1:24-32)

In popular culture it is all too easy to reserve talk about hell for the worst and most inhumane tyrants of world politics or perhaps for the serial murderers and rapists that get covered by the media. However, these words from the Bible might shock us: gossip, arrogance and envy are all deserving of death in the eyes of the Living God; they are all crimes against Him that prove the judgement of hell is upon us.

The hope of glory

The hope of heaven and the new creation future is given as a free gift in the Lord Jesus Christ, given to us simply when we put our trust in Him. This free gift through faith is nothing less than the 'hope of the glory of God'.

Jesus literally transforms His people from being God-hating addicts of evil destined for hell to righteous saints who are destined to be part of the divine life, sharing in the divine glory! Even now as we face hardship, loss and suffering, this hope of the glory of God keeps us going towards the glorious hope:

> Since we have been justified through faith, we have peace with God through our Lord Jesus Christ, through whom we have gained access by faith into this grace in which we now stand. And we rejoice in the hope of the glory of God. Not only so, but we also rejoice in our sufferings, because we know that suffering produces perseverance; perseverance, character; and character, hope. And hope does not disappoint us, because God has poured out his love into our hearts by the Holy Spirit, whom he has given us. (Rom. 5:1-5)

217

The new destiny that we are given in Jesus by the Spirit is bigger and more glorious than we can ever imagine. We are often told those mind-boggling statistics about the sheer size of the universe, with its billions of galaxies each of which is filled with millions of stars stretching across the second heaven in inconceivable distances. Yet, all of this, even up to the highest heaven that lies beyond and above the most distant galaxy, is straining forward in eager expectation for the destiny of the church to be fully and finally revealed at the appearing of Jesus Christ.

The whole universe has been placed under a deep curse of decay and frustration until the redemption of humanity has been completed, but the curse will be lifted and the universe will be suddenly and holistically released into the destiny that was planned for the entire heavens and the earth, planned from the eternal counsels of the Trinity in the endless ages before the creation of the cosmos.

Right now we still experience a world and bodies that are caught in the bondage of decay and frustration. Right now it is as if we are in a delivery room in a hospital maternity ward. The pain and the sweat, the spasms and the blood might seem terrifying, as if death is at hand – and yet the reality is that all the agony is about to give way to the ecstasy of the new born baby when pain is forgotten in the sheer joy of birth:

> I consider that our present sufferings are not worth comparing with the glory that will be revealed in us. The creation waits in eager expectation for the sons of God to be revealed. For the creation was subjected to frustration, not

by its own choice, but by the will of the one who subjected it, in hope that the creation itself will be liberated from its bondage to decay and brought into the glorious freedom of the children of God. We know that the whole creation has been groaning as in the pains of childbirth right up to the present time. Not only so, but we ourselves, who have the first fruits of the Spirit, groan inwardly as we wait eagerly for our adoption as sons, the redemption of our bodies. For in this hope we were saved. But hope that is seen is no hope at all. Who hopes for what he already has? But if we hope for what we do not yet have, we wait for it patiently. (Rom. 8:18-25)

The tension between this life and the next

Whether in life or in death, we belong to the Lord Jesus: we are never separated from Him, even though our bodies die:

If we live, we live to the Lord; and if we die, we die to the Lord. So, whether we live or die, we belong to the Lord. For this very reason, Christ died and returned to life so that he might be the Lord of both the dead and the living. (Rom. 14:8-9)

In 2 Corinthians 5 the apostle Paul presents one of the longest explanations of the tensions between living in this present life of suffering and wanting to leave this body to be close to Jesus in paradise. Paul has a short-term hope to be with Jesus when he dies, but his long-term hope is the great hope which is the final fulfilment and regeneration of all things at the final Day of God.

He explains how our mortal bodies may serve the glory of God even as we suffer and die. As we suffer loss for Jesus, as we deny our sinful desires, as we pour out our lives in love and service in our local church families, as we suffer persecution or even martyrdom for Jesus, so the eternal life of Jesus is displayed and even made available for other people.

All this is only possible because we keep our hearts and minds fixed on the unseen world above rather than the dying, seen world around us. Our inner life of the soul/spirit can get stronger every day, even as our outer bodily life is decaying away day by day. Though we live in a divided creation, cut off from the highest heaven, yet we set our hearts and minds on the resurrected and ascended Lord Jesus who is at the Father's right hand. Jesus is the unseen focus that captures us and draws us to Himself:

> We always carry around in our body the death of Jesus, so that the life of Jesus may also be revealed in our body. For we who are alive are always being given over to death for Jesus' sake, so that his life may be revealed in our mortal body. So then, death is at work in us, but life is at work in you. It is written: 'I believed; therefore I have spoken.' With that same spirit of faith we also believe and therefore speak, because we know that the one who raised the Lord Jesus from the dead will also raise us with Jesus and present us with you in his presence. All this is for your benefit, so that the grace that is reaching more and more people may cause thanksgiving to overflow to the glory of God. Therefore we do not lose heart. Though outwardly we are wasting away, yet inwardly we are being renewed day by day. For

our light and momentary troubles are achieving for us an eternal glory that far outweighs them all. So we fix our eyes not on what is seen, but on what is unseen. For what is seen is temporary, but what is unseen is eternal. (2 Cor. 4:10-18)

Why we're reluctant to leave

However, this is not the full picture – and Paul goes on to give us the rest of the story in the next chapter. The Biblical hope is not that we escape our decaying body and our 'immortal soul' floats away! That is the pagan thought of Plato! No, having shown us that by the power and grace of Jesus our inner life may flourish even when our bodies are dying, in 2 Corinthians 5 Paul goes on to fill out why we are actually reluctant to leave our dying bodies.

We were always created to be body, soul and spirit all wrapped up together as a single unity. We were never intended to experience life away from our bodies – and that kind of 'naked' existence, without the clothing of our bodies, can only ever be a temporary solution. It is great to be with Jesus, even if that means spending some time 'naked' without a body, but our true hope is to be **like** Jesus – clothed with His immortality and resurrected body, sharing the fullness of life in His new creation future:

Now we know that if the earthly tent we live in is destroyed, we have a building from God, an eternal house in heaven, not built by human hands. Meanwhile we groan, longing to be clothed with our heavenly dwelling, because when we are clothed, we will not be found naked. For while we are in this tent, we groan and are burdened, because we do not wish to be unclothed but to be clothed with our heavenly dwelling, so that what is mortal may be swallowed up by life. Now it is God who has made us for this very purpose and has given us the Spirit as a deposit, guaranteeing what is to come. Therefore we are always confident and know that as long as we are at home in the body we are away from the Lord. We live by faith, not by sight. We are confident, I say, and would prefer to be away from the body and at home with the Lord. So we make it our goal to please him, whether we are at home in the body or away from it. For we must all appear before the judgment seat of Christ, that each one may receive what is due him for the things done while in the body, whether good or bad. (2 Cor. 5:1-10)

A 'house' in heaven

Our physical body has become a mortal body, 'an earthly tent'. We live in this earthly tent but we have another dwelling – a house – in heaven. What is this house? Paul seems to be referring to the resurrection body of the Lord Jesus Himself. That immortal body, that eternal **house** rather than a temporary **tent**, was raised up from the dead, not by human hands but by the omnipotent power of God.

We are uneasy about losing this earthly tent because we were never designed to be naked. We were never intended to spend any time outside our physical dwelling.

But when?

Is Paul suggesting that we receive our resurrection body as soon as we die? Is he saying that as soon as we leave this earthly tent we will be resurrected into the heavenly, eternal dwelling?

It is true that the unique resurrection body of Jesus Himself is in the heavens, at the right hand of the Father, but the Bible teaches that the time of resurrection is at the very end, on the Day of Judgement when everybody is resurrected together.

When we die, when we are carried to paradise by the angels to join in fellowship with the church triumphant, we will see the resurrection body of Jesus at the centre of paradise and we will long for that final day even more than we do now. We will enjoy His presence and the fellowship of the church in an 'unclothed' state and we will cry out 'how long, O Lord?' until everything is put right (Rev. 6:10).

The 'Jerusalem above'

Paul talks of that 'Jerusalem above' in Galatians 4:26, picking up the confident hope that runs all the way through the Hebrew Scriptures. Though we are fragmented into all the different cities and kingdoms of this passing age, yet as we are included in the local church communities around the world so we are citizens of the city with foundations, the Jerusalem 'above'. That Jerusalem is founded on the free grace of God in Jesus rather than the human efforts and genetic divisions of this passing age.

In one of the most remarkable passages in Paul's letters the apostle claims to have literally been to that heavenly Jerusalem, the third heaven, the paradise of God. So extraordinary is this experience that he has to almost distance himself from it:

> I must go on boasting. Although there is nothing to be gained, I will go on to visions and revelations from the Lord. I know a man in Christ who fourteen years ago

was caught up to the third heaven. Whether it was in the
body or out of the body I do not know – God knows. And
I know that this man – whether in the body or apart from
the body I do not know, but God knows – was caught up to
paradise. He heard inexpressible things, things that man is
not permitted to tell. I will boast about a man like that, but
I will not boast about myself, except about my weaknesses.
(2 Cor. 12:1-5)

The mind boggles as we try to imagine what happened to
Paul and we need to be thankful he said no more than this!
Too many of us have already been overly fascinated with
these items of mere curiosity.

It is interesting that Paul doesn't know whether he
was in the body or out of the body when he was taken to
paradise. The very fact that he has no problem with the idea
of consciously existing outside his own body is important
because some people argue that the Bible never speaks of
such a state of existence for humanity.

We can only wonder why the Holy Spirit enabled Paul to
go on this incredible journey to the third heaven, but surely
the apostle was deeply encouraged in his sufferings, having a
further confirmation that whether he lived on in the body or
left his body in death, he would always enjoy the fellowship
of Jesus and His church:

I eagerly expect and hope that I will in no way be ashamed,
but will have sufficient courage so that now as always Christ
will be exalted in my body, whether by life or by death. For
to me, to live is Christ and to die is gain. If I am to go on
living in the body, this will mean fruitful labour for me. Yet

what shall I choose? I do not know! I am torn between the two: I desire to depart and be with Christ, which is better by far; but it is more necessary for you that I remain in the body. Convinced of this, I know that I will remain, and I will continue with all of you for your progress and joy in the faith. (Phil. 1:20-25)

Wanting to be with Jesus

Paul is genuinely torn between wanting to die to be with Jesus in paradise and staying alive in service for the church here. Remaining in the body was better for the church for that time, but as far as Paul was concerned departing from the body to be with Jesus is 'better by far'.

This is one of the strongest examples of longing for the intermediate hope in the whole Bible: longing not so much for the final resurrection hope but for the short-term hope of going to be with Jesus when we die.

Longing for His appearing

Nevertheless, it is not the temporary departure of Paul that ultimately drives him on, but rather than final appearing of Jesus on the day of judgement. In 2 Timothy when Paul is getting ready for his departure from this mortal body, he is looking beyond his stay in paradise to that final day when Jesus the righteous Judge will make everything right and reward His people:

For I am already being poured out like a drink offering, and the time has come for my departure. I have fought the good fight, I have finished the race, I have kept the faith. Now there is in store for me the crown of righteousness, which the Lord, the righteous Judge, will award to me on that day – and not only to me, but also to all who have longed for his appearing. (2 Tim. 4:6-8)

This powerful phrase captures a deep aspect of Paul's doctrine of the church – 'all those who have longed for his appearing'. This is the hope that sustained Paul in his final days.

We find the same hope in the earliest days of his letter writing, right back in the letters to the Thessalonians.

The Thessalonians were a raw new local church. They had been shown how Jesus was the long-promised divine Messiah of the ancient Hebrew Scriptures and they knew that He was turning the world upside down (Acts 17:6). They were attacked with savage hostility by the city officials who wanted to keep everything exactly as it was (Acts 17:1-9). How dare this church speak about another King, when the Roman emperor was the only king!

Paul was only with the Thessalonian church for about a month, so when he wrote to them it was essential that he gave them a better understanding of the way that the Lord Jesus was going to complete His mighty revolution of turning the world upside down.

Down the ages churches have sometimes tried to change the world in their own strength. Paul had to make it very clear that the revolution of Jesus was not like anything in this passing age.

This King is concerned with the whole created order, from the highest heaven down to the realms under the earth, bringing total justice and righteousness to the whole world. The greatest threat facing them is not the violence of a Roman emperor but the much more serious anger that God will bring down on the world on that final day of total revolution, the Day of Judgement:

> … you turned to God from idols to serve the living and true God, and to wait for his Son from heaven, whom he raised from the dead – Jesus, who rescues us from the coming wrath. (1 Thess. 1:9-10)

> May he strengthen your hearts so that you will be blameless and holy in the presence of our God and Father when our Lord Jesus comes with all his holy ones. (1 Thess. 3:13)

What about those who have died already?

If we are waiting for the day when Jesus returns to this world, then what about those who have already died? Will they miss out?

If all the action is going to happen **here** on planet earth, then what of the Christians who have died and left it behind?

Will they have to live on a lower level of 'ghostly' life in the coming age of glory? Will they be left in that half-finished 'naked' condition forever and ever?

> Brothers, we do not want you to be ignorant about those who fall asleep, or to grieve like the rest of men, who have no hope. We believe that Jesus died and rose again and so we believe that God will bring with Jesus those who have fallen asleep in him. According to the Lord's own word, we tell you that we who are still alive, who are left till the coming of the Lord, will certainly not precede those who have fallen asleep. For the Lord himself will come down

from heaven, with a loud command, with the voice of the archangel and with the trumpet call of God, and the dead in Christ will rise first. After that, we who are still alive and are left will be caught up together with them in the clouds to meet the Lord in the air. And so we will be with the Lord forever. Therefore encourage each other with these words. (1 Thess. 4:13-18)

Paul's words are such a wonderful comfort. Those who have fallen asleep in Jesus will be returning with Him when He comes back. They will be the very first to receive their resurrection bodies on that great day, returning with Jesus in the clouds of glory. When the final trumpet sounds and the archangel gives the mighty shout of triumph, dead Christians will be the first to rise. Then those who are still on the earth will rise to meet up with the whole church together in the air.

The greatest reunion of all time

The greatest reunion of all time will happen in the heavens as we all return to the earth together – our final home with Jesus forever and ever.

I'm sure, like me, you have often imagined what it will be like meeting up with Jesus and the entire church of every age in the heavens, watching as the heavens and the earth are purged with fire and regenerated into the new heavens and earth of the age to come.

Paul clearly thought a great deal about that resurrection morning and looked forward to seeing the true glory and worth of the churches, revealed for the miraculous wonder that they are:

For what is our hope, our joy, or the crown in which we will glory in the presence of our Lord Jesus when he comes? Is it not you? Indeed, you are our glory and joy. (1 Thess. 2:19-20)

The final day

So, when will all this happen?

Can we fix the date of this, even in broad terms? Could we at least fix a year to it even if not the exact day?

The apostle Paul rejects all this kind of speculation. The disciples had tried to get this very sort of information from Jesus, pressing Him on it as He was about to ascend into heaven. But even Jesus Himself was not concerned with times and dates. If the Lord Jesus Christ, the eternal and infinite Son of the Father, is content to leave all such matters in the Father's hands, then so must we:

Now, brothers, about times and dates we do not need to write to you, for you know very well that the day of the Lord will come like a thief in the night. While people are saying, 'Peace and safety', destruction will come on them suddenly, as labour pains on a pregnant woman, and they will not escape. But you, brothers, are not in darkness so that this day should surprise you like a thief. You are all sons of the light and sons of the day. We do not belong to the night or to the darkness. So then, let us not be like others, who are asleep, but let us be alert and self-controlled. For those who sleep, sleep at night, and those who get drunk, get drunk at night. But since we belong to the day, let us be self-controlled, putting on faith and love as a breastplate, and the hope of salvation as a helmet. For God did not appoint us to suffer wrath but to receive salvation through our Lord Jesus Christ. He died for us so that, whether we are awake or asleep, we may live together with him. Therefore encourage one another and build each other up, just as in fact you are doing. (1 Thess. 5:1-11)

We must live each day with total readiness for the final day. Whether that day comes today, next year or not for another thousand years, each church is to be ready. When it comes it will be like a thief taking the world by surprise. But while the world is sleeping, the church is awake and eagerly alert, keeping watch for the return of Jesus.

We know that at any time that divine Sun will rise and the eternal day will begin. We keep ourselves ready by throwing off the evil and selfish ways of the darkness, knowing they will all soon perish with the darkness:

May God himself, the God of peace, sanctify you through and through. May your whole spirit, soul and body be kept blameless at the coming of our Lord Jesus Christ. (1 Thess. 5:23)

That final day of justice will overturn the values of this passing age. Right now the Church is dismissed, mocked and persecuted, but on that day Jesus Christ will bring trouble to those who have so troubled the church. After it there will no longer be any confusion between good and evil, between the world and the church, because all those who do not obey the gospel will be forever shut out:

All this is evidence that God's judgment is right, and as a result you will be counted worthy of the kingdom of

God, for which you are suffering. God is just: He will pay back trouble to those who trouble you and give relief to you who are troubled, and to us as well. This will happen when the Lord Jesus is revealed from heaven in blazing fire with his powerful angels. He will punish those who do not know God and do not obey the gospel of our Lord Jesus. They will be punished with everlasting destruction and shut out from the presence of the Lord and from the majesty of his power on the day he comes to be glorified in his holy people and to be marvelled at among all those who have believed. This includes you, because you believed our testimony to you. (2 Thess. 1:5-10)

Judgement for the church?

The day of justice will mean permanent destruction and exclusion for the forces of evil, yet even for the church on that day there is kind of judgement or assessment of all that we have done.

Though we will be forever with the Lord Jesus, gathered into the great assembly, yet we will see our lives for what they really have been. If we have wasted our time investing in what is worthless or fleeting, then we will have little to show of lasting, eternal value. If we have invested in **people**, poured out our lives in local church service and life, then we will find the eternal, heavenly value of that love and self-sacrifice. The treasures (money, status, pleasures, possessions etc) of this present darkness will burn up like paper or hay on the day of God, but the treasures of heaven (church, character, love etc) will endure into the ages of ages:

By the grace God has given me, I laid a foundation as an expert builder, and someone else is building on it. But each one should be careful how he builds. For no one can lay any foundation other than the one already laid, which is Jesus Christ. If any man builds on this foundation using gold, silver, costly stones, wood, hay or straw, his work will be shown for what it is, because the Day will bring it to light. It will be revealed with fire, and the fire will test the quality of each man's work. If what he has built survives, he will receive his reward. If it is burned up, he will suffer loss; he himself will be saved, but only as one escaping through the flames. (1 Cor. 3:10-15)

Judge nothing before the appointed time; wait till the Lord comes. He will bring to light what is hidden in darkness and will expose the motives of men's hearts. At that time each will receive his praise from God. (1 Cor. 4:5)

Living with the seriousness this demands

This connects to the practice of discipline in our local churches. As we live in the light of that coming day when everything is revealed and properly valued, so we take our lives together with the proper seriousness that this demands.

If one of the church family refuses to turn away from the corruption of sin and threatens to pollute the body, it is vital that we expel them, even if that means great harm for them in this life. Even if Satan were to kill the excluded brother or sister, it is better for this to happen if they will turn from their sin and find eternal salvation in Jesus on that final day.

It is a most solemn thought. Do we really see the power and authority of the local church in these eternal ways? Do we live with such a sense of the coming day of judgement and truth that we hold each other to the light of that day even now in this mortal life?

> Even though I am not physically present, I am with you in spirit. And I have already passed judgment on the one who did this, just as if I were present. When you are assembled in the name of our Lord Jesus and I am with you in spirit, and the power of our Lord Jesus is present, hand this man over to Satan, so that the sinful nature may be destroyed and his spirit saved on the day of the Lord... I am writing you that you must not associate with anyone who calls himself a brother but is sexually immoral or greedy, an idolater or a slanderer, a drunkard or a swindler. With such a man do not even eat. What business is it of mine to judge those outside the church? Are you not to judge those inside? God will judge those outside. 'Expel the wicked man from among you.' (1 Cor. 5:3-5,11-13)

The hope of that day determines our lives today. The spirit of the age might make us think that we can do whatever we like with our bodies, that there is no ultimate meaning or value in what 'consenting adults do in private', but the light of that day shines on the local church and we encourage each other to keep it always in mind:

> The body is not meant for sexual immorality, but for the Lord, and the Lord for the body. By his power God raised the Lord from the dead, and he will raise us also. (1 Cor. 6:13-14)

> In the presence of God and of Christ Jesus, who will judge the living and the dead, and in view of his appearing and

his kingdom, I give you this charge: Preach the Word; be prepared in season and out of season; correct, rebuke and encourage – with great patience and careful instruction. (2 Tim. 4:1-2)

The way we think of and use our bodies comes from our future hope.

If we know that these bodies are for the Lord Jesus and that they have an everlasting holy future in His service then we cannot allow them to be used for sinful purposes. Our bodies – even these decaying and dying mortal bodies – must be used to the glory of God. The world might view anything other than a supermodel body as unworthy or unlovely, but when we are united to Jesus our bodies are given a resurrection hope that is almost too wonderful to believe:

> Our citizenship is in heaven. And we eagerly await a Saviour from there, the Lord Jesus Christ, who, by the power that enables him to bring everything under his control, will transform our lowly bodies so that they will be like his glorious body. (Phil. 3:20-21)

The hope of the resurrection body

The hope of the resurrection of the body comes to its fullest expression in 1 Corinthians 15 when the apostle Paul demonstrates with rigorous clarity the centrality of the resurrection hope for the life of the church.

If there is no physical resurrection at all, then the Lord Jesus Christ Himself is not risen; preaching and faith are useless; the witnesses that Jesus appointed are false witnesses;

the followers of Jesus are still in sin; dead Christians are lost forever; the church is full of the most miserable people!

However, if Jesus really has risen from the dead, then He is the first fruits from the dead – the first harvest of the much larger crop of the rest of humanity; the kingdom will be fulfilled and handed back to the Father, so that even God the Son will enter into His rest; the Lord Jesus will finally reign over all His enemies; death itself will be defeated; baptism makes sense; and we can risk our lives for the kingdom

Bodily resurrection?

The 19th century atheist Robert Ingersoll attacked the idea of bodily resurrection at the return of Jesus:

> Does anybody believe in bodily resurrection who has the courage to think for himself? Here is a man, for instance, that weighs 200 pounds and gets sick and dies weighing 120; how much will he weigh in the morning of the resurrection? Here is a cannibal, who eats another man; and we know that the atoms you eat go into your body and become a part of you. After the cannibal has eaten the missionary, and appropriated his atoms to himself, he then dies, to whom will the atoms belong in the morning of the resurrection? It has been demonstrated, in so far as logic can demonstrate anything, that there is no creation and no destruction in Nature. It has been demonstrated, again and again, that the atoms in us have been in millions of other beings; have grown in the forests and in the grass, have blossomed in flowers, and been in the metals. In other words, there are atoms in each one of us that have been in millions of others; and when we die, these atoms return to the earth, again

appear in grass and trees, are again eaten by animals, and again devoured by countless vegetable mouths and turned into wood; and yet the church solemnly tells us that it believes in the literal resurrection of the body. This is almost enough to make one despair of the future – almost enough to convince a man of the immortality of the absurd.[1]

The question about the ownership of atoms is one of the most common objections to the resurrection even today. Many people seem to think that we get a set of atoms and hold on to them throughout our lives and we should have the same set of atoms when Jesus resurrects everybody. I find that slightly strange because under atomic theory our bodies are a constantly shifting collection of atoms anyway, but it is something that people ask.

In a sense this question, and others that are like it, amount to asking how the LORD God will handle all the practical difficulties of resurrecting bodies that have long since decomposed back to dust.

How exactly will Christ raise everybody from the dead?

If the bodies have decomposed and dissipated across the world, how can those bodies be resurrected? Most of the bodies of the human race no longer exist, so how can they be reconstituted? Jesus' own body did not decompose, so it seems more straightforward to resurrect it, but what of the bodies of those who are long dead? Questions as to the mechanics of the general resurrection at the end of the world stretch back to ancient history, and we find them going on in this verse:

---

1. A lecture by Robert Green Ingersoll in 1884, entitled 'Death blows at Orthodoxy', Haldeman-Julius Publications (1950).

But someone may ask, 'How are the dead raised? With what kind of body will they come?' (1 Cor. 15:35)

Back to the beginning

To understand the end of the world, Paul returns to the beginning:

> …someone may ask, 'How are the dead raised? With what kind of body will they come?' How foolish! What you sow does not come to life unless it dies. When you sow, you do not plant the body that will be, but just a seed, perhaps of wheat or of something else. But God gives it a body as he has determined, and to each kind of seed he gives its own body. (1 Cor. 15:35-38)

It is foolish to worry about how our current bodies will transform into resurrection bodies when the world around us was created to teach us how to think about resurrection – 'What you sow does not come to life unless it dies.' (v. 36).

Jesus used the same feature of creation to explain His own resurrection in John 12:24. If we look at a seed and then look at the plant it will become, we should be constantly amazed. A small, shrivelled, dry seed goes into the ground and falls apart, yet out of that 'death' a wonderful, living plant emerges. God created the world in such a way that we would be constantly surrounded with these examples of our future resurrection.

God's 'acre'

The Lord God has a 'future body' ready for every seed. When we look at the seed itself we might find that hard to imagine

– we might well be amazed that the future body of an acorn is a mighty oak tree.

> When you sow, you do not plant the body that will be, but just a seed, perhaps of wheat or of something else. But God gives it a body as he has determined, and to each kind of seed he gives its own body. (1 Cor. 15:37-38)

What do you think of when you see a cemetery? What does it look like to you? The Puritans used to call a cemetery 'God's acre', because they grasped this. They saw fields full of seeds waiting to grow up into resurrection bodies.

If we are concerned about the mechanics of our future resurrection, we need to take time to plant some seeds and wait! Take time to learn the lesson that our heavenly Father built into the world.

Suitable bodies

> All flesh is not the same: Men have one kind of flesh, animals have another, birds another and fish another. There are also heavenly bodies and there are earthly bodies; but the splendour of the heavenly bodies is one kind, and the splendour of the earthly bodies is another. The sun has one kind of splendour, the moon another and the stars another; and star differs from star in splendour. So will it be with the resurrection of the dead. (1 Cor. 15:39-42)

If our Almighty Father was able to create all the different bodies in the first place, without using any atoms or matter of any kind, then how can we ever doubt His ability to create suitable bodies in the future? Doubts about our resurrection future always go hand in hand with doubts about the creation of the world. How can a person worry about the allocation of atoms, when the Trinity created all things without any atoms at all? It is so ridiculous.

People sometimes worry about the biological and physical processes of life in the new creation: the processes of death and decay are so essential to the basic processes of life in this fallen age of the creation, how can life go on without them? What kind of ecology could there be if the animals do not eat one another? What kind of physics can there be in a deathless new creation?

These worries are less about the mechanics of getting a resurrection body, and more about the mechanics of living in the new creation. Paul points us to the way that God has given suitable bodies to all the different creatures in the universe.

A fish has a body that is perfectly suited to its environment. It can breathe in water and move about with great efficiency. A fish out of water is hopeless, because it has been designed so perfectly for its own native environment. We might find it very hard to imagine how to live in an underwater environment, and yet our wise Father has designed bodies suitable for the fish.

The same is true of birds in the air and animals on the ground. Each has a body designed for the area that it has been placed in. It is able to adapt to and thrive in its specific environment. If the Father, Son and Holy Spirit were able to do all this, it makes no sense to doubt Their ability to do it for the renewed creation.

Heavenly bodies

Paul lifts our vision higher to even greater bodies:

> There are also heavenly bodies and there are earthly bodies;
> but the splendour of the heavenly bodies is one kind, and
> the splendour of the earthly bodies is another. The sun has
> one kind of splendour, the moon another and the stars
> another; and star differs from star in splendour. So will it
> be with the resurrection of the dead. (1 Cor. 15:40-42)

We might be able to cope with water, air and earth environments, but what about the heavens above us? Think of the scale and grandeur of the heavens. How difficult it must be to thrive in such an environment! Yet, the Living God has created bodies that are suitable even for such glorious locations. The sun, moon and stars were all made to thrive in their native environment.

If such wonders have already been achieved by our majestic Father, then we can rest in peace about His ability to raise us with glorious bodies suitable to the inconceivable glory of our future in the new creation.

Spiritual bodies

> So will it be with the resurrection of the dead. The body
> that is sown is perishable, it is raised imperishable; it is sown
> in dishonour, it is raised in glory; it is sown in weakness,
> it is raised in power; it is sown a natural body, it is raised
> a spiritual body. If there is a natural body, there is also a
> spiritual body. (1 Cor. 15:42-44)

We look at our mortal bodies: they are perishable, weak and return to the earth from which they were made. If we allow ourselves to be hypnotised by these facts we fail to see what these bodies will one day become. They will be imperishable, glorious, powerful and no longer made of dust. By the power of Jesus' resurrection, the natural body will germinate into the spiritual body.

Notice that the resurrection body is a perfect harmony of the physical and the spiritual. It is a **spiritual body.** It is not mere spirit, like a ghost – but a solid, physical body that is fully integrated with the heavenly realms. It is hard for us to fully comprehend such a glorious body.

All the concerns about our future resurrection bodies arise because we see that our bodies were created from the dust and return into dust. That is what Ingersoll was really worried about with all his talk of atoms. Created from earthly atoms, the body disintegrates back into nothing but atoms. Our future resurrection bodies have a different origin completely.

In the likeness of the Second Adam

Our mortal bodies are made from the dust of the earth, but our immortal bodies have a more glorious origin:

> If there is a natural body, there is also a spiritual body. So it is written: 'The first man Adam became a living being'; the last Adam, a life-giving spirit. The spiritual did not come first, but the natural, and after that the spiritual. The first man was of the dust of the earth, the second man from heaven. As was the earthly man, so are those who are of the earth; and as is the man from heaven, so also are those who are of heaven. And just as we have borne the likeness of the earthly man, so shall we bear the likeness of the man from heaven. (1 Cor. 15:44-49)

Formed from the dust of the ground, Adam was given some life by the glorious Lord of life. Adam was created mortal. The life he had been given could be taken from him. He was warned of the danger of death even before he became mortal. Adam was a living being made of dust.

Contrast him with the Second Adam, the Lord Jesus Christ. He is a life-giving spirit. Adam **received** life, but it was the Lord God who **gave** him that life. Adam was created from the dust, but the Lord God is from everlasting to everlasting. The eternal Son became flesh and dwelt among us – but His origin is the infinite life of God.

The man of the dust was lent life by the everlasting Lord of life, the Man from Heaven.

Just as with the seeds, the lowly comes first and then the glorious. Adam came first, but we should not think of him as the destination of humanity. He is the acorn, but Jesus is the mighty oak:

> The first man was of the dust of the earth, the second man from heaven. As was the earthly man, so are those who are of the earth; and as is the man from heaven, so also are those who are of heaven. And just as we have borne the likeness of the earthly man, so shall we bear the likeness of the man from heaven. (1 Cor. 15:47-49)

We are all born from Adam, our long-distant ancestor. We are all from the dust of the earth, and therefore we return to the dust and give back the life that we have borrowed from the Author of life. Just as Adam died and his body has long since disintegrated across the world, so too will our bodies – unless Jesus returns first.

However, if we belong to Jesus, if we have received a second birth in Jesus, then we already share the life of Jesus. The origin of Jesus is the immortal life of heaven at the Father's side. His resurrection life cannot disintegrate into the dust of the earth. The Son of Man is from heaven not from the dust. His destiny is glorious life not decomposition.

Jesus' resurrection body is founded on the immortality of the Living God. Jesus is the **author** of life not the **borrower** of life. Just as Jesus rose from the dead with a physical body that cannot ever be touched by mortality, so too will all of us if we have entrusted ourselves to Him for life and death.

Waiting – and working

We can only live as self-sacrificial disciples of Jesus when we live in the clear knowledge that our bodies will follow the pattern of Christ:

> Therefore, my dear brothers, stand firm. Let nothing move you. Always give yourselves fully to the work of the Lord, because you know that your labour in the Lord is not in vain. (1 Cor. 15:58)

We see whether a Christian really trusts in the resurrection future when we see how they pour out their life in the service of the gospel.

Through His death and resurrection, Jesus has opened the way for the seeds of our mortal bodies to flower into the glorious, spiritual bodies of the new creation. That is what we were originally created for and it is such a wasteful tragedy when anyone refuses that future.

All has been paid for, all has been prepared. All that remains is for us to receive that guaranteed future from Jesus the risen Lord.

CHAPTER 10

THE BEGINNING...

THE book of Revelation is such a treat for Bible-lovers, filled with reflections and quotations from all of the Bible. In it we find themes and images from nearly every other book, yet the great theme, as it is of the whole Bible, is the glory and victory of Jesus Christ, the Lamb of God.

The popular idea is that the book of Revelation is only about the end of the world, about the final day of judgement, the 'apocalypse' – the final state of hell and the renewed creation. Yet, this book was revealed to John by Jesus as an explanation of the whole of history from that moment right through to the end and into that new creation future.

See how the book begins:

> The revelation from Jesus Christ which God gave him to show his servants what must soon take place. (Rev. 1:1)

This is a revelation from God the Father to God the Son for the benefit of the servants of Jesus. It was given so that we would understand the whole of history from now and on into eternity.

Revelation will not only teach us what the final new creation will be like and what is to happen to death and Hades at the very end, but it will also teach us what is going on in history and in heaven right now.

As we have worked our way through all the Scriptures we have seen that there is a constant focus not only on the distant future but on heaven right now, as we look up to our Father in the throne room of heaven, the Zion that is above, the Mountain of God.

The First and the Last

The book begins by showing us who is going to bring history to its conclusion: the One who holds all authority and power over all the people in the world. Jesus frequently refers to Himself as the Son of Man and on two occasions overtly states that He is the Son of Man who will come on the clouds of glory (Matt. 24:30; 26:64; Mark 13:26; 14:62). Revelation 1:7 commands us to remember the vision of Daniel, of Jesus coming with the clouds. And then we are to see the vision of Zechariah 12:10, of Jesus the Lord pierced in crucifixion. The Crucified Lord comes in the clouds of glory.

It is the crucified God who has all the authority and glory in heaven and earth, power to judge the nations and defeat all His enemies. Even the physical appearance of Jesus (Rev. 1:12-16) is so like the Ancient of Days from Daniel 7:9 that we must conclude He is of the very same nature as the Father.

When John nearly drops dead in the presence of Jesus (1:17), Jesus introduces Himself in terms that govern all we will hear: 'Do not be afraid. I am the First and the Last. I am the Living One; I was dead, and behold I am alive for ever and ever! And I hold the keys of death and Hades.'

All the matters of life and death are found in Jesus Himself. He is the Living One. Whatever happens to us when we die is found in Him, the One who is Master of life and death. Even Hades is opened and closed, used and judged, by Jesus.

Throughout the book Jesus Himself is the key to heaven and hell; death and Hades; the new creation or the lake of fire. Those who are faithful to Him are kept safe, now, through death and on into that glorious resurrection future. Those who oppose Him or ignore Him will all face Him in judgement and destruction.

Over and over again we see the day of judgement presented as the triumph of Jesus and His bride. Yes, the book of Revelation is full of blood and thunder, dragons and conflict, but its purpose is to show us the real direction and outcome of all history.

As the Church lives under attack and under pressure while we wait for the return of Jesus, we need to know that He reigns over all and He is unrolling history exactly as He wills, reigning on the throne of the universe with His Father in the power of the Spirit.

He will return!

Just as in the gospels, the glorious, victorious return of Jesus, the divine Saviour and warrior, is global, universal, historic, cosmic and final:

> The sky receded like a scroll, rolling up, and every mountain and island was removed from its place. Then the kings of the earth, the princes, the generals, the rich, the mighty,

and every slave and every free man hid in caves and among the rocks of the mountains. They called to the mountains and the rocks, 'Fall on us and hide us from the face of him who sits on the throne and from the wrath of the Lamb! For the great day of their wrath has come, and who can stand?' (Rev. 6:14-17)

The devil may seem to be on the rampage, yet he is bound in chains by the authority of Christ and he knows his time is short. If ten is the number meaning 'the sum total' in Scripture, and three is the number of completeness, then the fact that Christ reigns for ten times ten times ten years – a thousand years – tells us that even now Christ Jesus is enthroned in the highest heaven ruling over all things.

Revelation 20:2 tells us that Satan is bound, and even if he is allowed one final moment of opposition and deception at the very end, yet the devil and all his armies have no future but the lake of fire – the Gehenna that Jesus spoke so much about in the gospels:

The devil, who deceived them, was thrown into the lake of burning sulphur, where the beast and the false prophet had been thrown. They will be tormented day and night for ever and ever. (Rev. 20:10)

Christ Jesus is the divine bridegroom, the rider on the white horse, who on that great wedding day will also ride out to war, that final war when He will purge the universe of all His enemies so that it can be the home of righteousness forever:

I saw heaven standing open and there before me was a white horse, whose rider is called Faithful and True. With justice he judges and makes war. His eyes are like blazing fire, and on his head are many crowns. He has a name written on him that no one knows but he himself. He is dressed in a robe dipped in blood, and his name is the Word of God. The armies of heaven were following him, riding on white horses and dressed in fine linen, white and clean. Out of his mouth comes a sharp sword with which to strike down the nations. 'He will rule them with an iron sceptre.' He treads the wine press of the fury of the wrath of God Almighty. On his robe and on his thigh he has this name written: KING OF KINGS AND LORD OF LORDS... (v. 19). Then I saw the beast and the kings of the earth and their armies gathered together to make war against the rider on the horse and his army. But the beast was captured, and with him the false prophet who had performed the miraculous signs on his behalf. With these signs he had deluded those who had received the mark of the beast and worshiped his image. The two of them were thrown alive into the fiery lake of burning sulphur. (Rev. 19:11-20)

So what is Hades?

When we looked at the teaching of Jesus in the gospels we saw what He meant by Gehenna, the final place of rejection and destruction, but what does He mean by this word 'Hades'? Jesus speaks about Hades in the gospels as well as here in Revelation:

And you, Capernaum, will you be lifted up to the skies? No, you will go down to Hades. If the miracles that were performed in you had been performed in Sodom, it would have remained to this day. (Matt. 11:23 and Luke 10:15)

And I tell you that you are Peter, and on this rock I will build my church, and the gates of Hades will not overcome it. (Matt. 16:18)

In Hades, where (the rich man) was in torment, he looked up and saw Abraham far away, with Lazarus by his side. (Luke 16:23)

Because you will not abandon me to Hades, nor will you let your Holy One see decay. (Acts 2:27 – quoting Ps. 16)

This verse is especially important because in the Hebrew of Psalm 16:10 we find the word Sheol (see also Acts 2:31).

I am the Living One; I was dead, and behold I am alive for ever and ever! And I hold the keys of death and Hades. (Rev. 1:18)

I looked, and there before me was a pale horse! Its rider was named Death, and Hades was following close behind him. They were given power over a fourth of the earth to kill by sword, famine and plague, and by the wild beasts of the earth. (Rev. 6:8)

Hades comes close behind death, as if the two are closely related:

The sea gave up the dead that were in it, and death and Hades gave up the dead that were in them, and each person was judged according to what he had done. (Rev. 20:13)

Hades does not hold on to the dead forever but has to give up the dead so that they can be judged:

> Then death and Hades were thrown into the lake of fire.
> The lake of fire is the second death. (Rev. 20:14)

Hades itself does not last forever but when it has given up its dead, it too is judged and destroyed.

Hades, then, is the same place that in Hebrew is called Sheol. When we studied Sheol from the Pentateuch and in the Psalms of the sons of Korah we saw that it is the place that fallen, sinful humanity naturally go to when we die.

Yet, all those who trust in Christ are redeemed from Sheol and taken up to Zion, the City of God, the Mountain of the LORD. In the light of the Old Testament, we can understand what is being said here in Revelation.

Jesus has the keys to Sheol/Hades and anyone who trusts in Him need not fear the grave. Jesus redeems His people from Hades. Luke 16:22-23 tells us directly how Hades/Sheol is the destination of the wicked but the righteous are redeemed from Hades as soon as they die:

> The time came when the beggar died and the angels carried him to Abraham's side. The rich man also died and was buried. In Hades, where he was in torment, he looked up and saw Abraham far away, with Lazarus by his side.

The same lessons – different images and symbols

The book of Daniel is filled with dreams and visions that teach the same lesson over and over again. Daniel is shown how the Son of Man, Jesus Christ, rules over history with a kingdom that outlasts all the little kingdoms and empires of this world.

Nebuchadnezzar's dream of a statue of four materials in Daniel 2 taught this, but the same lesson is taught in a different way when Daniel dreams of the four beasts in chapter 7. The ram and the goat in chapter 8 teach us the same thing again from another angle and so again with the vision of all the kings in chapter 11. Daniel shows us the meaning of history, what is always going on behind the scenes and how it will all end, in several different visions, dreams and incidents.

So too with the book of Revelation. When the great visions begin from chapter 4 we are shown the victory of Jesus over all His enemies using different images and symbols. The Lamb triumphs; the Kingdom of heaven conquers the kingdoms of the world; Babylon falls and the Church is married to Christ; the dragon is imprisoned and then finally cast out forever. Again and again we see the same final triumph of Jesus over all His enemies.

Think of the structure of the book. Jesus shows John the Revelation and dictates seven letters (chapters 1-3). Then we are shown the throne room of heaven where only Jesus, the Lamb that was slain, is able to unlock the meaning of history, the scroll with its seven seals (chapters 4-7).

Another way of seeing the pattern comes next as seven trumpets are sounded as a warning to the world in chapters 8-11, reminding the world of the final judgement to come. Chapters 12-14 show us history and the future in terms of the ongoing conflict in the heavenly realms between the devil and the Church, telling us that we do not war with flesh and blood but with spiritual forces that are defeated by the preaching of the gospel.

Chapters 15-16 shows us the sovereignty of the heavenly throne room with the seven bowls of final judgement poured out on to the earth. Chapters 17-19 give us another image for understanding the triumph of Jesus through history: the fall of Babylon, the city that represents human pride and idolatry. The end of chapter 19 gives us another image, this time of Christ leading the armies of heaven to destroy the devil and his armies. Chapter 20 is yet another vision, this time showing how Satan is imprisoned even now and will finally be cast into the fire.

The book ends up with a glorious vision of the new creation future, centred on Christ and the church, free from all enemies for ever and ever.

Letters of endurance

Jesus, who appeared to John on Patmos as the First and the Last, the holder of the key of death and Hades, writes seven letters to churches, challenging and encouraging them to stay faithful to Him right to the end. The ending of each one is so significant.

The tree of life

> To him who overcomes, I will give the right to eat from the
> tree of life, which is in the paradise of God. (Rev. 2:7)

If Hades is the place that the wicked go when they die, the righteous are redeemed from Hades and taken by the angels to paradise, as was promised to the thief who died next to Jesus in Luke 23:43. It is the place that Paul visited in 2 Corinthians 12:4, the third heaven, where he heard things that cannot be spoken. We will see a lot more of paradise in chapters 4-5, but for now we are told that the tree of life that had been in the Garden of Eden is now held within paradise.

Jesus ends the curse and exile that drove Adam and Eve out of the Garden of God.

All that the Garden of Eden was is now held in paradise, in heaven with the Father, awaiting the day when it will come back down to earth, with the city of God, when the heavens and the earth will finally be re-united together as one.

The second death

> … you will suffer persecution for ten days. Be faithful, even to the point of death, and I will give you the crown of life. He who has an ear, let him hear what the Spirit says to the churches. He who overcomes will not be hurt at all by the second death. (Rev. 2:10-11)

In Scripture, the number ten means the total sum; the full amount. (The ten commandments are the full summary of the commandments.) So, here, to be persecuted for ten days means the full amount of persecution. It means death, as becomes clear in verse 11. Even though we die in the service of Jesus, yet there is a crown of life for us. That will be the final enemy we face. Death can never touch us again once we have died in this life.

Though our enemies may kill our bodies, yet they can do no more than that. Matthew Henry says, 'If a man is kept from the second death and wrath to come, he may patiently endure whatever he meets with in this world.'

The second death is mentioned again in chapters 20-21.

> Blessed and holy are those who have part in the first resurrection. The second death has no power over them... (Rev. 20:6)

> Then death and Hades were thrown into the lake of fire. The lake of fire is the second death. (Rev. 20:14)

> The cowardly, the unbelieving, the vile, the murderers, the sexually immoral, those who practise magic arts, the idolators and all liars – their place will be in the fiery lake of burning sulphur. This is the second death. (Rev. 21:8)

This second death is what Jesus meant by the word Gehenna in the gospels. Though the wicked may be held in Hades until the final judgement, when Christ comes in all His power and glory, with all His holy angels with Him, then even Hades itself will be judged. Then, when everything is thrown out into the lake of unquenchable fire, it will be the second death.

A new name

> To him who overcomes, I will give some of the hidden manna. I will also give him a white stone with a new name written on it, known only to him who receives it. (Rev. 2:17)

Isaiah 62 is a glorious chapter describing the new creation future of the church and in verse 2 the LORD declares, 'The nations will see your righteousness, and all kings your glory; **you will be called by a new name** that the mouth of the LORD will bestow.' That new name turns out to be *Hephzibah* meaning 'my delight is in her' – and a new name will also be given to the land itself: 'Beulah', meaning 'married'.

The new names for the church and the creation show that our ultimate future is all about the wedding feast of the Lamb and the marriage that goes on into eternity.

This new name is secret, yes, because the world thinks the church has no future and is simply to be despised. The true identity and destiny of the church as the bride of God in the home of righteousness are known to us but hidden to the world.

If the Promised Land is ahead of us, how can we be ever sure of getting there, with all the troubles, doubts and fears that surround us? How will we be sustained and guided through this wilderness so that we can finally cross the Jordan?

Just as our new name is hidden from the eyes of the world, so is the manna that daily sustains us. We look up to heaven now, each day, to give us the bread we need, the guidance and strength, the comfort and joy in this wilderness journey. We are also looking forward to that new creation future when we are married to the living God.

Listen again to who you are!

In Revelation 19:7 when the whole creation celebrates the fall of Babylon, the whole church shouts for joy:

> Let us rejoice and be glad and give him glory! For the wedding of the Lamb has come, and his bride has made herself ready.

That is when that new name is truly revealed.

The City of God, filled with all the saints who have died and been taken to paradise, must join with the saints who are still alive on that great day and in Revelation 21:2 that city of the triumphant saints in heaven comes down from heaven to the new marriage home – 'I saw the Holy City, the new Jerusalem, coming down out of heaven from God, prepared as a bride beautifully dressed for her husband.'

In Revelation 21:9, and right down to verse 27, one of the angels shows John that great city that is the Bride of Christ – 'Come, I will show you the bride, the wife of the Lamb.'

It is vital for us to read that description regularly. Our true identity is hidden and we may even forget it ourselves when the world, the flesh and the devil so frequently speak their lies into our hearts and minds. If we listen to those lies and start to think like a non-Christian about our true name, then we fall into the futile thinking and sin that will drag us down. No! Listen to who you are, *Hephzibah Beulah* – married to God who delights in you:

> 'Come, I will show you the bride, the wife of the Lamb.' And he carried me away in the Spirit to a mountain great and high, and showed me the Holy City, Jerusalem, coming down out of heaven from God. It shone with the glory of God, and its brilliance was like that of a very precious jewel, like a jasper, clear as crystal... (Rev. 21:9-11)

We will judge the world with Christ!

To him who overcomes and does my will to the end, I will give authority over the nations – 'He will rule them with an iron sceptre; he will dash them to pieces like pottery' – just as I have received authority from my Father. I will also give him the morning star. (Rev. 2:26-28)

When Paul first wrote to the Corinthians he was concerned that they were taking one another to court. I guess we've grown all too used to Christians doing that sort of thing, but the apostle Paul was deeply concerned about it because, as he says in 1 Corinthians 6:2, 'Do you not know that the saints will judge the world? And if you are to judge the world, are you not competent to judge trivial cases?'

Psalm 2 describes how Christ will destroy all those who oppose Him, all those who persecute His church – yet that work of judging the world is shared with us. Just as we live and reign with Christ right now in the heavenly realms, as Revelation 20:4 tells us, so at the end we will judge the world with Christ.

This too is an aspect of our future hope that needs to stay within our minds. It is all too easy to get involved in the same kind of arguments and fights that the world does. Remember that when Jesus was asked to arbitrate over a disputed will, with possibly large amounts of money in dispute, He said that it had nothing to do with Him. Can we see money and status and reputation in such a way? If we are going to judge the world, then we must be able to judge the simple matters of this passing age.

If we can jump to the last of these seven letters just for a moment we see that the same promise is given there too:

To him who overcomes, I will give the right **to sit with me on my throne**, just as I overcame and sat down with my Father on his throne. (Rev. 3:21)

It might seem strange to us that such a glorious hope is held before us. I sometimes have enough trouble managing the most simple hassles of day to day life, yet in Christ we are being discipled and trained to judge the world and reign with Him over the whole creation.

Even right now (Eph. 2:6) 'God raised us up with Christ and seated us with him in the heavenly realms in Christ Jesus'. This is such a strong encouragement for us to take responsibility in our lives and learn the self-control that the Spirit brings.

Rule the world with an iron sceptre? Can we really do this? No, of course we can't and yet in Revelation 2:28 He promises, 'I will also give him the Morning Star'. Christ puts us alongside Himself to reign and judge, but He first gives us **Himself**.

Christ is Himself the Morning Star, as Revelation 22:16 tells us. Even now as we study the Scriptures, Peter tells us that this Morning Star can rise in our hearts (2 Pet. 1:19).

We take responsibility and learn the maturity to judge and rule **NOT** by trying harder or putting more effort in, but rather by seeking, loving, trusting Jesus Christ, the bright Morning Star. Yes, our future is glorious, full of responsibility and work that we perhaps cannot yet imagine, but it is Christ Himself who takes responsibility for us and He leads us to sit with Him on the throne in the highest heaven.

White robes

He who overcomes will, like them, be dressed in white. I will never blot out his name from the book of life, but will acknowledge his name before my Father and his angels. (Rev. 3:5)

The hope of the church is not based on what we have done. If we are going to have secure confidence in our future hope we have to understand what guarantees that future. How could we ever find a place in the paradise of God? How could any of us ever be accepted in the presence of the Most High, where even the angels hide their faces as they declare the holiness of their LORD? Our hope of being received into paradise when we die and going on into that resurrection future is just the same as that thief on the cross who was guaranteed a place in paradise by Jesus. Jesus, the Lamb of God, gives us white robes made clean through His blood. He is the Shepherd who leads us and knows us in that majestic glory.

Revelation 7 shows us a vast crowd of Christians from both Old and New Testament times, all gathered in paradise around the throne of God:

> One of the elders asked me, 'These in white robes – who are they, and where did they come from?' I answered, 'Sir, you know.' And he said, 'These are they who have come out of the great tribulation; they have washed their robes and made them white in the blood of the Lamb'. Therefore, 'they are before the throne of God and serve him day and night in his temple; and he who sits on the throne will spread his tent over them. Never again will they hunger; never again will they thirst. The sun will not beat upon them, nor any scorching heat. For the Lamb at the centre of the throne will be their Shepherd; he will lead them to springs of living water. And God will wipe away every tear from their eyes.' (Rev. 7:13-17)

When the real history begins...

> Him who overcomes I will make a pillar in the temple of
> my God. Never again will he leave it. I will write on him
> the name of my God and the name of the city of my God,
> the new Jerusalem, which is coming down out of heaven
> from my God; and I will also write on him my new name.
> (Rev. 3:12)

Here we come to the great and final state of the universe –
the union of heaven and earth; the removing of the cosmic
curtain that hides us from the Father's face.

Those that overcome by trusting Jesus will be part of that
great re-ordering of all reality as the whole creation becomes
the home of the living God for ever and ever.

Notice here in Revelation 3:12 that we will be named
not only as the Church, the City of God, but also with the
name of God Himself and the new name of Jesus, the name
of the rider on the white horse that no man knows. This is
all telling us of that great and eternal union that will begin
between Christ and His bride when the real history of the
universe finally begins.

Whatever wonders we have ever dreamed or imagined
will be nothing but boring shadows when chapter one of the
history of humanity finally begins.

The heavens and the earth are new, as Revelation 21:1
tells us, not because they are annihilated and replaced with
different ones, but because they are so thoroughly re-ordered
that they are 'as new'. Think of the difference between the
oak tree and the acorn or the caterpillar and the butterfly.
They are the same organism, yes, but they are also new in

so many ways. All that is in the finished form is there in the seed, but when it is shown in its full grown glory it seems so much more.

When we see the resurrection body of Jesus at the end of the gospel stories we see how the continuity is there. He eats and drinks; He talks and walks; He cooks breakfast and enjoys friendship… and yet, He has passed into such a different order of life and being that He can no longer just stay here among us as before.

He has taken His place sharing the throne of the universe so that the whole creation can follow Him through into that undiscovered country of the resurrection.

> Then I saw a new heaven and a new earth, for the first heaven and the first earth had passed away, and there was no longer any sea. I saw the Holy City, the new Jerusalem, coming down out of heaven from God, prepared as a bride beautifully dressed for her husband. And I heard a loud voice from the throne saying, 'Now the dwelling of God is with men, and he will live with them. They will be his people, and God himself will be with them and be their God. He will wipe every tear from their eyes. There will be no more death or mourning or crying or pain, for the old order of things has passed away.' He who was seated on the throne said, 'I am making everything new!' Then he said, 'Write this down, for these words are trustworthy and true.' (Rev. 21:1-5)

Our mourning is all at an end,
When, raised by the life-giving Word,
We see the new city descend,
Adorned as a bride for her Lord;
The city so holy and clean,
No sorrow can breathe in the air;
No gloom of affliction or sin,
No shadow of evil is there.

By faith we already behold
That lovely Jerusalem here;
Her walls are of jasper and gold,
As crystal her buildings are clear;
Immovably founded in grace,
She stands as she ever hath stood,
And brightly her Builder displays,
And flames with the glory of God.

(CHARLES WESLEY, 1746)

APPENDIX:

ABSENT FROM THE BODY, PRESENT WITH JESUS

WE can see the new creation hope of cosmic resurrection ahead of us, yet most of us may face our own death before the day of Jesus' appearing. So, can we really hope for heaven when we die or should we think more in terms of coming back to life and consciousness only when that day of resurrection happens?

Do we consciously wait in paradise with Jesus until that final day of resurrection or are we all 'sleeping' in the grave till that final day?

Even in the New Testament we can see something of a theological argument between Sadducees and Pharisees about human life beyond death. Christians would never take the Sadducee view of no life of any kind beyond death at all, but there have been and still are Christians who believe that when our bodies die, we have no further conscious existence until the final day of resurrection.

For ease, we could summarise the three main views in this way.

First, there are those who focus on the idea that the human **soul** or **spirit** is the 'real person', the only bit that really matters. The idea is that the soul is essentially immortal and will exist in one way or another forever after the death of the body. After death the immortal soul will be taken up to heaven to exist in a disembodied state forever and ever, contemplating the wonder and beauty of God in the fellowship of the other dead souls and the angelic host.

In this view, there is little or no place for a final day of judgement or a future resurrection because the final state of the immortal soul is achieved as soon as we die. Death is to be seen entirely in terms of the 'death of the body' because the human soul cannot die. In the same way there is really no place for a renewal of this creation because the destiny of the immortal soul that trusts in Jesus is to remain in the highest heaven forever. Sometimes people who take this view speak about a totally different kind of 'spiritual' creation of the future, but there is no real future for these heavens and earth that we now know. The wicked are also immortal souls but at death they are immediately thrown into eternal hell: again, there is no real need for a final day of judgement in this viewpoint.

Second, there are those who take almost the very opposite view and say that the human **body** is the essential definition of human life. The idea of the human soul or the human spirit are ways of speaking about aspects of the human brain or human life that are completely tied to the human body. So, in this view [traditionally known as 'mortalism' or 'conditional immortality'], when the human body dies there is no ongoing human life at all. Bodily death is the end of existence for a human being. The future resurrection hope is the only possible kind of human life beyond the death of the body. When we die we would have no more consciousness of anything until we are all resurrected by the LORD Jesus on that final day – whether resurrected to everlasting life with Him in the renewed creation or resurrected to a 'second death' – the oblivion of annihilation – as the final punishment for sin. The second death, when the resurrected body of the unbeliever is killed, is the final end for the wicked and their consciousness and existence entirely ends [or is annihilated] at the second death. Whether this second death happens very quickly or more slowly is something that people vary about, but the end result is the physical death and therefore total annihilation of the wicked.[1]

However, as we have gone through the Scriptures in this book, it will be clear that we are not persuaded by either of these viewpoints. As we saw when we studied the Hebrew Scriptures, the most ancient church was convinced that the Lord God would deliver them from the power of Sheol and take them to be with Himself at the time of death. The idea that the Church was captured and held in Sheol just the same as the wicked would have been a terrible thought to the ancient church!

---

1. It has been argued that even the word 'soul' is a mistranslation of the Hebrew word 'nephesh' [which should be understood simply as 'life'] or the Greek word 'psyche' [which should be understood simply as 'mind' or 'life']. Furthermore, it may be argued that because the life or soul is in the blood [Leviticus 17:11], therefore when the blood stops flowing, so does the life.

Angels and demons are clearly described in the Bible – and yet they exist in a way that it is not based on the kind of physical or bodily life that we are familiar with. So, we cannot exclude the existence of intelligent, personal life beyond the physical body. Yet, we seem to have more than the angels and the demons have: we have the added glory of physical bodies, made from the dust of the earth itself. Just as the animals have the breath of life in them, so too does humanity. Creatures of the earth, we have life and breath, yet furthermore we were made to enjoy fellowship with the Living God in the highest heaven. It is as if the whole creation from top to bottom finds expression in the original design of human beings.

Just as the whole creation was originally created to be a unity of the heavens and the earth, with free access to the holy mountain of God in the highest heaven, so we too were created to be a harmonious unity of the spiritual and the physical, heaven and earth coming together in the human family. Yet, the curtain has fallen between heaven and earth; the fall has brought a profound division between heaven and earth. This division is experienced in our own existence when our bodies die and decay away. Death brings about the most strange and unnatural state for human beings: created to live as a harmonious unity of the whole creation, we find ourselves unnaturally torn apart in death. The natural fate of fallen humans is for our bodies to return to the dust and our souls or minds with our spirits to be left homeless and lifeless in the shadowy and fading world of Sheol or Hades.

Yet, part of the wonderful good news of Jesus Christ is that He does not leave His people to the lifeless shadows and corruption of Sheol. He takes us to be with Himself when we die, out of His sheer love and grace. Yes, we will still be waiting for that final day of resurrection when we are united back together as body, soul and spirit, but even that strange and unnatural life outside our bodies is redeemed and made glorious by the love of Jesus, the grace of the Father and the fellowship of the Holy Spirit.

The classic understanding of the Bible down the ages and around the world is that although we were designed to be a unity of body, soul and spirit, yet the Immortal God grants to humanity an ongoing but temporary kind of existence beyond the death of the body such that whether lost in the shadowy realms of Sheol/Hades or resting in the fellowship of the saints in paradise, all of humanity continues in conscious existence beyond the death of the body.

In other words, the Bible teaches that when we die we go either to Paradise with Jesus or Hades with the lost to await the final day of judgement.

The continued conscious existence of Moses and Elijah at the transfiguration of Jesus clearly demonstrates this, as does the wonderful promise that Jesus made to the dying thief – 'I tell you the truth, today you will be with me in paradise.' We have seen how Jesus in Luke 16, when explaining about the dangers of loving money, told how a rich man went to Hades after death whereas the poor man, Lazarus, went to enjoy fellowship with Abraham.

When we examined the teaching in the epistles we saw how the final hope of bodily resurrection did not rule out the shorter-term hope of being with Jesus when we die, while we wait for that day of resurrection.

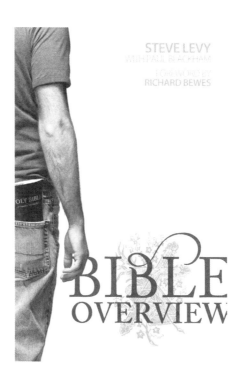

STEVE LEVY
WITH PAUL BLACKHAM

FOREWORD BY
RICHARD BEWES

BIBLE
OVERVIEW

Bible Overview

STEVE LEVY WITH PAUL BLACKHAM

With an evident love for the task, and with a delightfully light touch, Steve Levy wants to show us the glory of Christ and with plenty of fun along the way!

WILLIAM PHILIP,
Minister, The Tron Church, Glasgow

... Steve Levy fights back to reclaim a thrilling Bible that from beginning to end speaks of Jesus. If you want more joy in your Bible reading, if you want to love Christ more, read it!

MICHAEL REEVES,
President and Professor of Theology, Union School of Theology, Oxford

This is a page-turner of a book! I truly cannot think of a better way of introducing someone to the Bible than through these wonderfully luminous chapters.

RICHARD BEWES, OBE,
formerly of All Souls Church, Langham Place, London

That it is well written and easy to read is good for starters; but the heart of the situation is the sheer happiness of meeting someone who is so in love with the Bible, so sensible in his approach..."

ALEC MOTYER,
Well known Bible expositor and commentary writer

Steve has a fever for the Bible and is desperate to infect you! Let him.

DALE RALPH DAVIS,
Minister in Residence, First Presbyterian Church, Columbia, South Carolina

ISBN 978-1-84550-378-9

Christian Focus Publications

Our mission statement –

STAYING FAITHFUL

In dependence upon God we seek to impact the world through literature faithful to His infallible Word, the Bible. Our aim is to ensure that the Lord Jesus Christ is presented as the only hope to obtain forgiveness of sin, live a useful life and look forward to heaven with Him.

Our books are published in four imprints:

CHRISTIAN FOCUS

Popular works including biographies, commentaries, basic doctrine and Christian living.

CHRISTIAN HERITAGE

Books representing some of the best material from the rich heritage of the church.

MENTOR

Books written at a level suitable for Bible College and seminary students, pastors, and other serious readers. The imprint includes commentaries, doctrinal studies, examination of current issues and church history.

CF4·K

Children's books for quality Bible teaching and for all age groups: Sunday school curriculum, puzzle and activity books; personal and family devotional titles, biographies and inspirational stories – because you are never too young to know Jesus!

Christian Focus Publications Ltd,
Geanies House, Fearn, Ross-shire,
IV20 1TW, Scotland, United Kingdom.
www.christianfocus.com